COP IN *CRISIS*

TO

COP IN *CHRIST*

Detective Matt Thornton

My Father's Business Presents:

Title: Cop in Crisis to Cop in Christ

Publisher: My Father's Business

Author: Detective Matt Thornton

www.mfbyouth.org

Cover Photographer: Gina Fiene / www.fienephotography.com

Editing: K. Edmonds/N. Simmons for 21st Street Publishing Group

Typesetting/Cover Design/Self-Publishing Assistance:
21st Street Publishing Group / 21StreetUrbanEditing.com

ISBN No: 978-1-940097-57-2

LCCN: TBD

First Edition

2 4 6 8 10 9 7 5 3 1

TRIGGER WARNING: This book contains scenarios regarding, murder and suicide.

Printed in the United States

FOREWORD

Have you ever watched a really good movie, only to be told by someone that the book is even better? Well, this would be that book. I am not sure if there are plans to create a film based on this book, but I have no doubt it would have a lot of commercial success.

There is a saying that goes "Everything happens for a reason". Every now and then, an event will occur, or a person will come into our lives that reinforces that saying. When I was asked to write a foreword for this book, my initial reactions were of surprise and honor. At the same time, I wondered why I was chosen because prior to reading this book, I had not yet been introduced to the author.

Since then, Matt and I have spoken many times and I now consider him a good friend. How Matt and I crossed paths was actually by chance, or at least so I thought. The only obvious things I felt we had in common were that we are both in law enforcement. Matt is a detective for a suburban police department outside of Chicago. While I was born and raised on the south side of Chicago, my law enforcement career encompasses 29 years having worked in both Los Angeles County and the State of Hawaii where I am currently a Captain. I learned that neither of us grew up wanting to be police officers. After reading this book I learned that our reasons for not wanting to be were very similar.

Both of us grew up in an area where we had friends and family members who were on the other side of the law. We both have strong convictions for enforcing law the right way. We both have a passion for mental health awareness. And spiritually we both believe in a Higher Power.

Ultimately, as with most officers who choose this line of work, our decision to become public servants through the department was based on a higher calling. A calling to make a positive difference in the communities we serve.

After reading the first few pages of this captivating book, it started to become obvious to me why I was chosen to be involved in this impactful project. Not that I am necessarily more qualified than anyone else in this profession of ours, but quite simply because I was meant to be involved.

Call it fate, destiny, or divine intervention. Occasionally, events happen in our lives that we try and rationalize. It's part of human nature to try and put meaning as to why things occur. Sometimes the answer is not so apparent.

As one of several volunteer peer counselors for my police department, I can attest to the importance of mental health awareness for law enforcement personnel. This includes both sworn and non-sworn.

Somewhere, there is a strong-willed prideful officer desperately trying to cope with the many stressors of their job. This book happened for that reason. Somewhere, there is a dispatcher trying to cope with the fact that they are unable to receive closure on so many calls they send officers to respond to. This book happened for that reason. Somewhere, there is someone who is so depressed that they feel the only solution is to end it all. This book happened for that reason.

What I can say with absolute certainty is this book will take you on an epic thrill ride. The subject matter is timely and relevant. So, sit back and enjoy the ride.

I will end this with a quote from the book that really resonated with me. "I can never convince the streets to love the police but by my love and actions, I can convince them to love me and then convince them there are many others, just like me."

Captain Roderick Green has a total of twenty-nine years of law enforcement experience. Green is currently assigned as a Patrol Captain for the Kauai Police Department. He holds a bachelor's degree in Criminal Justice from Bethel University. Captain Green is a graduate of the FBI National Academy Class #270.

This book is

DEDICATED

to the ***loving memory*** *of*

Tyree Lavon Gulley

March 3, 1998 - April 13, 2019

Dear Matt,

I know you're having a rough time. I know God is on your side and this is just another task that He knows you are gonna get through. I know your job is harder than mine will ever be, but just know if you need me to come and just spend some time with you, I'll be there in a flash. I love you from the bottom of my heart, Matt. And I know with some prayers and a little faith we can overcome any problem. There are not enough words in the world to say how thankful I am that I met you. Keep working and try to stay stress-free and I'll do anything I can to help.

I always wanted to tell you, Matt, if it wasn't for you showing me the other way of life, I would have still been lost in the world. I wear my My Father's Business shirt every day when I work-out. I shed a couple of tears thinking about all you guys did for me. I don't know how to give all my thanks. Thanks for being a father type in my life even though you have kids of your own. You don't know what that means to me. Thanks for every step you took with me to change my life and still my life is changing every day. You, Lori, and Zach are my backbone. Every day that goes by I think about how much you guys changed my life and are still changing my life.

I don't want to be the one who doesn't get past the gates when it's time. I forever have that in my head. I want to start putting more items together for my story. I love you, brother. I can't wait to tell the world my story and to have you by my side. Can't be more blessed than that. I want to come ASAP. You don't know how happy I'll be to come tell people our story, how we got to know each other and how you guys helped me.

I'm ready to let the people hear our voices and our stories. Without any question, you will always and forever be loved by me.

Tyree

Dear Tyree,

I will see you when I get there. Then we can worship the Lord who saved us together forever. I love you, Tyree.

My strongest soldier ever.

No more pain.

I'll take it from here.

Your brother, Matt

Dear Brother or Sister in Christ,

First and foremost, I am not a writer.

As a matter of fact, I am a self-proclaimed, redeemed moron. If there is one thing on earth that I can tell you (besides Jesus is the only answer) it would be: never take yourself too seriously.

I have more flaws than you can possibly fathom. I've been a goofball from childhood and I'm that same goofball now. I decided to write this after much prompting from certain people that I could no longer deny. You see, when God talks to you, He usually does not audibly whisper into your ear.

He uses people to speak for Him.

So, after the last verification from my big brother, George Moore Jr., who told me to write, I figured I'd better, because God kept using people to encourage and speak this to me.

I am an extremely simple man. Give me a workout regiment, a tattoo chair, and some protein bars, and I'm good to go. I barely passed high school, was a horrible student, never went to college for a single minute, and cannot tell you what an ACT test looks like.

My father is of Irish descent and my mother is of Mexican descent, so I am an Irish Mexican American who never really knew where I fit in. I never felt Mexican enough and never Irish enough.

I know race and ethnicity are hot topics these days. I know there are many half and half readers out there that can relate and while I love both of my heritages, neither entirely define me.

I see all human beings as being created in the image of God. I wish we all would.

I just love everyone the same.

I was named after the first Gospel and my grandfather, the first Tejano, to watch every Cubs game ever played.

I have a horrible temper and cry real tears over my sports teams and the movie, Brian's Song.

I have four biological children - three awesome girls, and one awesome son.

I am the adoptive father to hundreds of other children, and I wouldn't have it any other way.

I am not only a detective, I am also the CEO of the world's most awesome outreach program that has blown up more than I could have ever imagined.

When you hear the letters MFB (My Father's Business) in my city, know that you are hearing something that is literally the divine work of God.

While most kids dream about being a cop as a small child, being a cop was the last thing I ever imagined. It was the opposite for me growing up. I hated police with a passion. I had numerous negative run-ins with them growing up. And now that I know the rules of engagement, I know for a fact that there were incidents along the way that were abuse of power. Those kinds of incidents can have a long-lasting effect and for some, those instances of abuse of power can have a lifetime effect.

I have done what some would consider wretched and horrible things in my life. I am literally an open book with no room to condemn any living, breathing human being - well, except for the guy who invented the Real Housewives franchise. Being that I have a house full of females, the Housewives shows have impeded on my football and baseball watching privileges far too many times.

It took me thirty-seven years to be drawn to my only hope of living. He was an ancient King from the middle east. You may have heard of Him. His name was, and is, to come.

If you've read this far, thanks, and I love you. Here are the thoughts of a saved, bald, class clown, cop.

Enjoy.

LETTER

Dear World, Winter, 2013

I want to leave this so that there are no questions about my intentions. For those of you who only know me as Matt, the class clown and may be shocked by this act, you'll know the truth now.

I wanna apologize to those who loved me. I wanna say fuck you to those who didn't. I don't how I got to this point, but I'm here. The numbness that I feel every day is finally about to come to an end.

To my kids, you are the most awesome gifts and the greatest babies who ever existed. I hope that you will forgive me one day, but I don't expect you to.

To Icemic, Lori, Big Show, Joanie, and Pops - I love you. There was nothing that you could have done to stop this so don't feel guilty.

To *XXXXX*, I want you to know that it's fuck you forever. You were never nothing but headaches for my life and you made it as difficult as you possibly could, so now live with this reality.

Bury me in a Cubs jersey.

At my service, I want two songs. "I Can Only Imagine" and "Prodigal Son".

I don't want any police procession, bagpipes, and there better not be one single cop there. You punks never did anything to help me and I wish I had just stayed my ass at a normal job.

Joanie, don't worry about me. I'll be with your mom and Melanie.

Love,
Matt

JANUARY 2013

Cop In *Crisis* to Cop In *Christ*

It was one of the last nights in January. I had started my usual midnight shift. I was driving alone, listening to my favorite song on repeat.

"I wake up in the morning and I ask myself, is life worth living should I blast myself? Before I go to sleep at night I ask myself, is life worth living should I blast myself..."

The entire song is about a guy debating whether to shoot himself in the head.

I sang along and felt every single word of that song.

I played that song out in my head hundreds of times.

I'd listen to that song some days for eight or nine straight hours and cry to myself. This was my life, my daily routine.

It had been so long since anything made sense to me. All I knew was that I wanted out of my pain.

The pain of my failures.

The pain of this life lying to me.

I thought life was supposed to come together when I got a career. The pain of being punked into serving the false god of worldly gain. The pain of knowing what I had done to my kid's lives. They watched me do so much evil in their short little lives.

I practiced by putting my little KelTec inside of my mouth to see how I would grip it to make sure I did the job right. I couldn't mess it up and risk maiming myself. It had to be done just right to make sure...

On this night, my plan seemed so close, so real, inevitable. I decided that I would use a towel to cover my head. *That will make for a clean crime scene, and at least, my brother Mic will not have to look me in the face.*

I had done nothing but cause trouble living at his house, the legendary 735, our address on College Avenue.

He used to call me Jack Tripper from Three's Company because every weekend, I ended up waist deep in trouble. Many drunk nights of stupidity, hedonism, debauchery, and misery. I must have brought legions of demons into that house with me. My bad, Mic. And I probably still owe you a couple of months of rent, too.

I pulled over on Wadsworth and 41 to write my last note and final goodbye out of this darkness on the iPad2 that my mom bought me for Christmas.

I hated myself and my first wife.

I hated the backstabbing bullies in blue.

I never realized what a cutthroat business policing would turn out to be. Alpha males who always need to one up and gain any advantage they can on you. I hated God for not fixing all of this and taking away this pain.

Why do I cry so much?

Why does everything I touch turn foul?

Why does nobody notice all this pain I'm in?

Am I really nuts?

Don't get me wrong, I knew God existed. But after so many years of darkness, I had blocked Him out in my mind.

My suicide letter was a short summary of my pain – who I hated the most, who I loved the most, and the request that absolutely no police officers be allowed at my funeral.

My mindset was that they never understood me and failed at their attempts to brainwash me.

One final betrayal by my sergeant was just about as much as I could take.

I won't even lie, I fantasized about taking him out just before I took myself out. I guess I answered my own question. *Yes, I am nuts.*

The letter detailed my funeral songs as well. For some reason, I've always been obsessed with music, even up to the point of planning for it after my death.

So now I only needed to take this letter and leave it where someone would find it, and then do the deed. This was my plan. One to the inside of the mouth and the rest would be history. I was all set. Dwelling on it.

How will I hold the gun?

How will I lay down?

Or will I be sitting up?

Should I just cover my head with the towel and then make the one last call?

The last call would be to my current girlfriend. But this time, I'd gone too far and hadn't talked to her in a long time. One last goodbye would have to do it.

It was windy, about two o'clock in the morning and about ten degrees below zero. I hated winter, but hey, I would never have to see another one after my plan was carried out—the silver lining.

I was parked in an empty parking lot, crying while staring at my steering wheel. I remember counting the tears as they fell one by one onto my pant legs. It seemed like I was the only person in all of Zion awake at such a late hour.

Out of the corner of my eye, I saw a lady who worked at the store walk out into the parking lot to her car. I watched her reach in and grab something from the inside. She started toward me, and I instantly got pissed.

Why would she or anyone come out in this ridiculous cold? I have nothing to say to her and I definitely don't want to talk to anyone. I tried to wish her away so I could finish my plan and cry in peace. But sure enough, she made a beeline straight to my squad car.

It was ridiculously cold and the wind was blowing. Her long black hair blew sideways as she approached. I had no choice but to wipe my tears away and look up. I rolled the window down about three inches, enough for her to unexpectedly stick her hand in to give me something.

I reached up to grab whatever it was she was passing through the slightly cracked window of my cruiser. It was a red cross.

"You need to have this," she said.

Then she immediately turned around and walked away. No explanation, no look back, nothing.

I was so confused.

She had stopped me in my tracks.

It took me a few moments to gather my thoughts and realize what had happened. I'm here prepping how to blow my own brains all over my lap...

The lowest I have ever been in my thirty-seven years on earth…

Then, some strange lady comes up to me at 2 a.m., in horrific weather that no human being should ever choose to walk in, with a cross.

"You need to have this…"

For seemingly, no reason at all.

Okay, Matt. What the hell just happened?

I'd never felt anything so ironic and surreal.

For a moment, time slowed. I sat and stared at the cross, baffled. Within seconds, I felt like something supernatural happened.

I clutched the cross and actually looked up as if I was going to see God's face, hovering over me.

Call me nuts or crazy or whatever you want, but I then screamed out loud. Like a loud, audible scream, toward the roof of my squad car.

"God, I know you're there! Please do something! I'm about to die! Please save me!"

And this is the part where people think I'm definitely crazy.

Christ answered me back.

I still to this day can't tell you if it was audible, in my mind, or both.

But I know what I heard.

He told me that He knew everything that I'd done.

He said that the reason He died was because He loved me enough to take my punishment.

He said to stop what I was doing.

He said He would forgive me.

He said to just follow Him.

After I heard those words, I felt this unexplainable peace come over me.

It was unlike any feeling that I had ever experienced in my life.

It was as if a fog had been lifted.

I felt hope and light for the first time in longer than I could remember.

The tears in my eyes were poured out like buckets. I was in a total state of shock. The rest of the night is a blur until the sun came up.

I believe I just found a dark place to sit and cry and wonder what in the world just happened to me.

I was terrified. How in the world would I explain to people that I just heard Jesus talk to me. Absolutely no one on earth would believe me.

****

I waited and waited for a close co-worker to come into work to start her shift. I hadn't heard from her in weeks, so I wasn't even sure if she would speak to me.

I cornered her in her squad car in the police department's east lot. I started to talk to her, but I couldn't stop crying.

One of the few times in my life, I was unable to spit out one single word. She was probably thinking the worst happened. When I was finally able to talk, I told her that something had happened to me that she would not believe.

I told her that I met Jesus and that I was in shock and then I begged her not to have me committed to a mental hospital.

She looked at me sideways and expressed her concern that I might be completely losing it this time. I assured her that my experience was true.

She said, "Okay," and then hugged me.

I told her I needed to go home and contact my sister, Lori, who worked for a church. So I went home and called Lori. She immediately set me up with Pastor George Shlief.

I had heard through the grapevine that Lori was very worried about my mental health and had been trying to get certain people to talk to me. So for Lori, I believe that was an extremely exciting phone call to make.

I remember walking in and sitting in his office, terrified, thinking about what I would say to him.

One of the first things he told me was that he'd heard all about me and my antics and that many people had been praying for a miracle to intervene in my life.

I told him that they got their supernatural occurrence.

I did not tell him the details immediately because I was afraid he would think I was crazy. I just told him that I had an encounter and that I wanted to do everything I could to follow Jesus from then on out.

This was when the old, dead Matt Thornton was resurrected.

In the Bible, you will see many references of people going from dark to light, from death to life, from flesh to spirit, from an enemy to a child of God, from blind to having sight…

Well, I think you get the point.

This was me.

The Lord chose for some unknown reason to resurrect me at that moment. I still have no explanation for why, but I am going to be obedient and go wherever He needs me to go. Little did I know that this was the beginning of what would become a mission that millions of people would find out about one day.

NOW WHAT?

At first, I was terrified to tell anyone what happened to me and it never crossed my mind for a second that literally millions of people would hear about it.

I really did hide this story for quite a while. I always put myself in someone else's shoes and if I heard that a suicidal cop claimed that he met Jesus in a parking lot, I would scoff and think that he is nuts. So this story took quite a while to come out.

Pastor George was very supportive of my new faith and taught me about anything I wanted to know. First and foremost, we dived into scripture.

I think a preconceived notion is that once you get saved, everything is gonna go your way. Like you ride off into the sunset and live your best life. That could not be further from the truth.

There was a reason Jesus said, *"In this world you will find trouble."*

I know this was not some figment of my imagination.

I know that Jesus somehow spoke to me.

Once that happened, I wanted to find out everything I possibly could about Him. I dove into my Bible and started to read often and most of all, I asked questions.

I remember finding out that you don't have to have some formal words to say to God, that you could literally just talk to Him, and that is a prayer. This blew my mind for some reason.

My daily routine now consists of having a running conversation with the Lord.

I remember asking Him over and over to please let me see the world like He saw it.

And also, of course, thanking Him for having a couple of spare minutes for me in the parking lot that night.

I didn't plan this type of thinking. The Lord just gave it to me. And that's exactly how He answered. There were many instances when He just showed me things.

I started to listen to some of my old demonic music and I remember not being able to get through thirty seconds of it without having to vomit. This is the music that encouraged me to blow my own head off.

The music that is a tool of the enemy, Satan. I simply put down my headphones and really had no music for quite a while.

Another thing He showed me was very simple, but quite effective. I remember having these unbearable urges to just talk to strangers. For some reason, my heart just bled for strangers. I wanted to tell the entire universe about this Jesus, who took so many years of an evil black fog depression and in one moment, made it all go away.

I want to shout, "Look what He gave me!" and "You can have it too!"

You could not shut me up about Jesus. It was like the more I chased after Him, the more I could feel myself wanting to take on His qualities and desiring to obey His commands.

A young Christian trying to navigate through a violent city on a nightly basis was interesting, to say the least. The very first thing I had to do was pretty much make a group announcement that I was retiring from debauchery. I think the fact that I was the most unlikely guy on the department to have something like this happen adds to my miracle.

People who know me now must understand that I set the bar for being a dog back then. I was the foulest-mouthed, porn-addicted, women-scheming, cheating, self-centered, hottest-tempered, scum bag in the department. There was not even a close second. I was the guy that when the police chaplain would do his ride-alongs, guys would tease and act like they were going to send them to ride with me, knowing that I would hate it. I was actually terrified of it.

Booze, women, and more women were pretty much my life. I had already destroyed my marriage from that combo and had no plans to stop until it killed me. And then the Lord showed up.

Kinda crazy, but I was terrified when I told the other cops. I knew they wouldn't believe me anyway and think it was another one of my pranks. It took a long time for them to see that this was for real. I started bringing a Bible to work and would read it when there was down time. My mother who we all call Joanie, bought me a bible when she heard what the Lord did. She wrote in the front cover,

For you, eternal joy.
January 31, 2013

I stopped participating in my old usual foul activities. I still got invited out for our old wild nights, but I had to turn that down.

The book of Ezekiel in Ezekiel 36:26, tells us that the Lord will give you a new mind and a new heart.

This is the supernatural that people don't really consider when the Lord saves. You can never take away the supernatural from God.

This was not Matt turning a new leaf or cleaning up his behavior. This was a dead Matt, becoming resurrected and made into a whole new person by the same spirit who raised Christ from the dead. It's pretty mind blowing when you sit back and think about it.

I kind of walked this challenging thin line of not wanting to come across as self-righteous, but very much wanting to chase Christ.

I was a very young Christian and did my best to navigate things. I then pretty much had to trust that God would handle the rest. Some people are gonna believe you and some will not. And that's perfectly okay with me if anyone is skeptical. I know the truth.

I believe this goes to show that the Lord will meet you exactly where you are.

Even in all of your sin and filth, He will stop you dead in your tracks and save you.

A lot of people think that you need to clean up first to be saved by Jesus. The truth is the exact opposite. That's why I can never judge anyone whatsoever and that's why I love speaking to unbelievers.

You never know when the Lord will move and the least likely most sinful person can be drawn to Christ.

To me, that is the most rewarding part of being a follower of the King – telling others His story.

That is why I can never shut my big mouth about Him.

SO, WHAT MAKES A COP HATE HIS LIFE?

I get that question all of the time.

I guess the answer can be quite complex with many facets.

But before I dive into those questions, I want to first maintain that I am not asking for sympathy and I am not excusing my suicide plan.

The fact is, what I had planned was pure madness and mental distress. It would have destroyed my children. It would have destroyed my immediate family, extended family, and all of those around me.

I always make it perfectly clear whenever I am asked…

Yes, if I would have carried out my plan, I would be spending my entire eternity in hell.

Period.

No feel-good clichés and no R.I.P.

Not because I committed suicide – because I would have died in my sins.

I had rejected Christ.

I had head knowledge because my parents taught me, but I had no true heart knowledge of Jesus.

I knew of Him, but I did not actually know Him.

I believe a lot of people get this twisted. Suicide is not an unforgivable sin. But dying without knowing and then trusting and believing in the atoning blood and grace of Christ is unforgivable. Scripture makes this very clear.

As I type this, I am coming home from the funeral of a friend who took his life exactly one week ago. I could not help but picture my own family standing over me distraught and never being able to ask me why.

Why did I not get help?

Why did I not tell them?

Why would I choose to leave my kids?

It was so eerie to be there and I felt such heartache for everyone who loved him. I will forever wish I could go back and have a conversation with him before he carried out his plan. I pray that my friend had true knowledge and belief in Christ. I pray that he had a weak destructive moment and is currently resting in Abraham's bosom.

So back to the main point of why a cop would hate his life so much. The main answer is, I was running from my creator as opposed to running to Him.

I took everything that accompanies having power and I used it for evil instead of good. I know, I know…

The first thing people think of is a dirty cop. I violated rights, hurt people or did illegal stuff. That could not be further from the truth. The fact is, I will stand before God one day and say honestly that I never hurt anyone or violated anyone's rights, ever, as an officer of the law.

Not one time.

I have never had one founded citizen complaint in eighteen years on the job.

What I did do, however, is use my power to access evil and chase any sin I could possibly chase. I was like a kid in a candy store of sin, with an ego the size of Jupiter. My goal in life was to set the bar for hedonism. I wanted to be the best at being the foulest. And I did a very good job of it.

If you are reading this and the only Matt you know is after January of 2013, then you have never met this unrecognizable Matt.

I chased nothing but sin for years and years of my life. I could write an entire non-fiction book series on my path of destruction. But in a nutshell, it led me right up to the edge of putting a gun in my mouth and doing the unthinkable.

UNLIKELY COP

M*y journey to wearing* a badge is probably about as unlikely as any you will hear. I never aspired to be a police officer. It was nothing I dreamt of as a child or even thought of. I actually disliked the police passionately growing up. I remember believing that 95% of cops were out of touch, White, racist, egomaniacs.

What molded my thinking was a combination of the handful of encounters that I had with cops when I was younger and what I saw around me while growing up.

I grew up in a predominantly white town called Winthrop Harbor, Illinois. It sits on the northern border of Illinois, right between the city of Zion, Illinois and the city of Kenosha, Wisconsin.

I didn't interact with a Black child until I was in my freshman year at Zion Benton High School, Since Winthrop Harbor was too small to have its own high school, high school kids were bussed to neighboring Zion.

Winthrop Harbor was a town that was known as a racist town. I really couldn't tell you where this started or if there is even any truth to it but possibly it was because there didn't happen to be any Black homeowners in the town, or Black kids in any of our schools.

When I got to middle school, I noticed I was a little different because I was half Mexican. I'm not saying that I was discriminated against or bullied. I remember just feeling like a normal kid. But I also specifically remember a lot of racist ways about the Harbor. I recall specific incidents with leaders of schools, to local police officers, to your run-of-the-mill citizens, almost celebrating that there were no minorities in the Harbor.

I'm not in the business of throwing people under the bus, but let's just say there were people with racist attitudes who were in positions of leadership that absolutely should not have been.

It is rumored that the KKK was prevalent in the 70s and 80s in Winthrop Harbor. I have never studied Harbor history, but I can tell you that this was the prevailing mindset.

Black people stayed out of our town and did not go north of Zion out of fear of violence or persecution.

As a juvenile, I saw KKK graffiti on our bike trails and I personally witnessed Black kids get chased out of the town. I also witnessed a Hispanic family, that lived five houses down from mine, have *Get Out* spray-painted on their home. It seemed that at that time, when you saw a vehicle stopped in the Harbor, there was a 95% chance that the driver was Black and just traveling north, trying to make it through town to the northern Illinois border to cross over into Wisconsin.

My little mind had a very hard time processing this. As a young child, my ideals were highly driven by what the society I knew taught me.

Black people were to be strangers.

Black people were to be feared.

Black people should stay out of our town; and, our town is better because of it.

These were the sickening ideals I was shown communally by Winthrop Harbor growing up.

Now, before I bad mouth the Harbor anymore, let me tell you that things have changed for the better. Every year, I am ecstatic to say there are a large amount of Black and Brown faces in the Harbor. Winthrop Harbor now seems to be embracing diversity, but the history doesn't change. So I am simply painting you a picture of what I saw as a child.

It also seemed to me that police profiling was extremely disproportionate growing up. I remember as a kid my little mind's view was, "If you are Black or Brown, you don't stand a chance."

Going into my freshman year of high school, I played football and basketball. This is when I had my first experiences with Black kids. I can tell you from the bottom of my heart, that I was immediately embraced and loved by them. They all befriended me. They all protected me.

I remember a specific incident my freshman year of high school, probably within the first month of school.

I had a really pretty girlfriend who all the older guys tried to pick up. I was tiny and shy and terrified to stand up to anyone.

One day in the lunchroom, the nose tackle of our football team, Dewayne Peet, caught wind of these bullies. I remember he grabbed me and said, "Come on with me."

He marched over to the bullies and stood over the entire table of about five or six dudes. He then proceeded to threaten the entire table with permanent physical damage should they ever say a word to me or my girlfriend for the rest of their lives.

I remember the faces on these bullies fill with complete terror, as Big Peet was one of the top five toughest kids I'd ever met.

Not one of them even looked my way ever again. And if they had decided to, Big Peet would have made sure they got accustomed to a hospital food diet.

Now as a terrified kid, these things make such a huge impact on your life. Turns out that the more love I got from Black people, the more I realized just how much I'd missed out growing up in my town. I thought back on a lot of the racist things I saw as a child, and I became extremely bitter and angry towards any form of bigotry.

Actually, I was pissed off.

Why aren't my friends allowed in my town?

Why aren't these kids embraced?

Why did the police seemingly pick on Black people?

This thinking was later verified as I matured right in the middle of the Rodney King incident.

Now if you are too young to remember the Rodney King incident, it happened in Los Angeles when a Black motorist was beaten half to death on camera by White officers.

The video was made public and even Helen Keller could have determined that the responsible officers should have been incarcerated for years. However, that did not happen.

They got off scot-free.

Not guilty.

After the officers were found not guilty in the trial, Los Angeles blew up into riots. I remember my sister showing me the newspaper article when the riots had started. I was sixteen years old, and I remember it like it was yesterday.

I was so angry that I said, "F?*k those racist. I hope they tear that f&*kin' city up."

This was when my abhorrence of police pretty much kicked into full gear. When I say I hated police, I really mean that. I had this evil disdain toward them in my heart that was at an extremely inappropriate level.

Justice? They called this justice?

I was so hurt for my Black friends. I couldn't imagine the hopelessness that they felt, like they could just be subject to beatings and death with no repercussions from our government.

This was around 1991-1992. It resonated with me for a long time. This, and what I saw growing up is what molded the way I thought about police officers in general. So when I say that I am the least likely person who would be an ambassador for the police, I absolutely mean it.

****

I was never a good student in high school and proudly finished in the bottom ten percent. My goal was just to stay eligible so that I could play sports. I was good at football, one of the best baseball players in my class, and I was the starting point guard my senior year in hoops. Being that I was a little rebellious punk, I didn't play baseball past my sophomore year even though I had been named the MVP of the team.

Sorry to Mr. Bee, our varsity baseball coach; we had a great team, too. He told me years later, still with a pissed off look on his face, "We were a Matt Thornton away from going down state in '93."

My bad, coach! I was going through some things as a kid. I still regret that to this day.

I remember having to get a fifty percent or higher on my chemistry final in order to walk the stage for graduation. The grade of D-minus was my goal for every class I took. I had about as much ambition as the slime that a slug leaves when it crawls across the front stoop.

I always tell kids I speak with, "Do not follow my example!"

A.C.T.? S.A.T.? What are those? Never took one.

I was by some miracle able to squeak by and walk the stage, though. A rebel, check that – a runnin' rebel – up until the day I left.

I recall wearing my UNLV jacket over my graduation gown. My daddy is from Las Vegas and we were raised on UNLV so all you posers who copied Tupac better turn your *Starter* gear in to me, you wannabes!

Following high school, I had zero plan. I was a bum for the better part of two years and then I went on to get a job with a local company, driving a fork truck. Total check-to-check, blue collar work.

Now as I had mentioned earlier, I was a rebellious and angry young man. I had quite the hateful temper and an extremely loudmouth. There were a few situations that I had gotten myself into during my late teens that were pretty dangerous now that I look back.

As an angry young man, I remember my older brother bringing home his first firearm. I held that .9mm and felt powerful and tough, like most angry young men would.

I have to get me one of these! I remember thinking. I ended up purchasing my own gun shortly after that. I also remember getting in quite a few situations involving that gun. Looking back, I see that for reasons now known the Lord protected me. He was setting me aside for something later in life. I feel very fortunate that I didn't get myself killed back then.

One night I was pulled over for speeding in my old drop top Cutlass. The officer ended up locating that loaded gun, illegally hidden in my glove box. I was taken into custody and charged with felony unlawful possession of a weapon. Not one of my finer moments. I sat in the County Jail overnight until I was luckily able to get bonded out the next morning.

Being shackled and at the mercy of a judge is something that opened my eyes a great deal. I remember telling myself that I would never ever come back to this place. I ended up pleading guilty to a misdemeanor and got supervision. The conviction will always be on my record, and it hindered me a great amount in my future endeavors. But I'm here now, writing this, so I guess it goes to show that no mistake you've made can stop God's plans for your life.

1998

O***n May 5***, 1998, my life forever changed in the most beautiful way.

Monique Thornton was born to me.

Man, to see that big old head pop out of that little opening in the birthing room. I almost puked and passed out, but I stuck it out.

My Momo!

May 5th forever became Cinco de Momo.

My first born.

My best friend.

My baby girl.

My heart.

My soul.

My pain in the a$$.

My little monster.

My mini twin.

Being a father is the best thing that can possibly happen in a man's life. And although Momo had colic for the first four months of her life, which was equivalent to Chinese water torture while being whipped with razors, she settled down and became an energetic little terror.

She was officially the worst behaved infant in human history and I loved every second of it. I mean, it's no exaggeration that she was horribly out of control.

This little animal needed a leash 24 hours a day. From the time she could crawl, she was destroying things.

Anyone that knows me knows that I react in the opposite of most everyone because, well, I am a moron like I said (shoulder shrug). I thought her antics were absolutely hilarious. Nobody would babysit her. She would hit, bite, scream, destroy.

If you've seen the movie scene from the '80s version of King Kong, when King Kong was locked in the boat and just pounded away at everything in a tantrum. This was my Momo every hour of every day.

I remember my sister, Lori, calling me and complaining while babysitting.

"Come get this animal!" she screamed into the phone.

I instantly started laughing. Apparently, she had destroyed her grandma's Christmas tree, pulled the whole thing down. Grandma Joanie wanted her ejected, umpire style!

My little Momo got run like Billy Martin out of her grandma's house. At the stores, she would immediately scamper away if you left her alone. I am ashamed to say that we lost her quite a few times in public.

I ended up marrying Momo's mother, Monica. We got our first house right down the street from my mother's home. Luckily, that gun charge didn't cost me my job. I was officially a family man. And although I hated my warehouse job, it paid the bills.

Unexpectedly, Monica became pregnant again. Momo was going to turn two almost exactly at the due date. They told me that I was going to have another girl, even though I did not want another girl. What man wouldn't want a son when he already had a girl.

I accepted it and picked out more pink baby stuff. This time we would name our daughter Madeline. It was similar to my name, Matt, so I thought it would be a good name. There would be Matty, which my brother calls me, and Maddy.

We had two ultrasounds and both times the doc said, "Yup, that's definitely another girl."

Let's move on to May 9, 2000, four days after Momo's second birthday. Labor time. Monica had a really long and difficult labor the first time around and this time would be no different.

There was no internet back then, so it was crossword puzzles and newspapers to read for all those hours in the birthing room. I went through the process of watching the whole thing again, still just as gruesome, but I still didn't puke.

So, this little head pops out the same as the first time. Then the shoulders and little butt. Looked exactly like Momo! Then the doc turns the little butt over… and I saw a little weenis and patunas!

I have a boy!

"I have a boy!"

I literally screamed and jumped up and down. I screamed into the hallway. I jumped up and ran through the hallway. I had to be told to calm it down a little by staff.

No way! I have a son. I have a son. I have a son!

The most surprising and blissful second of my life was seeing him flipped around like that. What a shock. Well, it was the easiest decision I ever had to make.

He would be called Matthew Junior.

Little Matt.

MJ.

My partner.

My ride or die for life.

This one wasn't as smooth as the first one, health wise. Junior ended up having some health issues but made it out of the woods after spending the first six weeks of his life in Children's Memorial Hospital.

Then we got home and ugh, colic kicked in. Another four months of torture but this time, with Momo standing by to add salt to the razor lashings.

Of course, we couldn't leave Momo alone with Junior because for some reason, she felt the need to attempt to murder him every chance she got. She would just attack him for no reason at all, like a little psychopath.

Momo, when you read this, you owe me, Junior, and your mother a lifetime of free dinners and apologies!

Junior was no angel as an infant but paled in comparison to the antics of the original terrorist herself, my Momo.

Man, I love my two little morons more than any words could express.

So now with a family of four, I persisted on in my warehouse job.

I would make other money on the side when I could, but we were basically a simple lower middle-class family, surviving from check to check.

No shame in that.

I knew I wasn't going to be rich. No college for either of us parents, but we still provided a good life for our babies.

There were lots of good memories in our little shack on Whitney Avenue. I ended up getting hired by another company and made a little more money, probably like a dollar more an hour, and the hours were better. This was my life, twenty-one to twenty-nine.

It was during those years, I learned what hard work was like, and what the monotony of simple living was.

There was very little stress.

There was very little excitement, which I liked, and there was very little change.

2004

It was 2004, the year that I happened to see that two of my best friends become police officers. I thought that was pretty cool. I had Five-O friends now.

I used to bombard them with questions of what the job was like. They seemed to like it very much and we would talk about their duties and calls for hours.

Yes, I still had a dislike for cops in general, but the hatred had waned a little over the years. I hadn't had many run-ins with police in later years. Also, I never saw my buddies as cops. They were simply the same friends I had known all my life.

I remember asking them what the minimal qualifications were for becoming a cop and they told me a high school diploma was all you needed for most police departments.

But I would always be reminded of my gun charge. No police department would ever hire me with that on my record. Plus, add on the fact that Monica's brothers and many of my friends were street affiliated.

Before you smear or have any thoughts on gang members, let me tell you that these are some of the closest and best people I've ever had in my life. They always protected me with their lives and never let anything happen to me. To this day, I would lay down my life for any of them. I love them with all of my heart. I have no problem stating that and I'll take whatever heat that brings. I will never back away from that.

I remember sitting in the break room at my job and seeing in the newspaper that Waukegan Police Department was hiring officers. Sure enough, all they required was a high school diploma. I never in a million years saw myself as an officer. Growing up with such a dislike for them and seeing them as mostly racist bullies, I just couldn't quite picture it.

But then I saw what the starting pay was and I was kind of shocked. It was way more than what I was making, like double my salary actually.

Why not take the test? What in the world do I have to lose?

I filled out the application and took the test for the Waukegan Police Department. I remember thinking to myself, *Man, I hope they don't ask who my family is.* As much as I loved them and still love them to this day, they were pretty notorious in Waukegan. I ended up taking the physical and written test along with a couple hundred other people. I thought to myself that it was a fun day, but there was no way I'd make it through all of the hurdles. This will be something that will come and go and then I'll get back to my real job.

Weeks went by before I received a letter in the mail from the Waukegan Police Department. It read that there were around a hundred and twenty applicants that made the list and their rankings were listed in numerical order.

I purposefully read the list from bottom to the top because there was no way I could be ranked that high. Heck, I was shocked that I actually passed the test and was even reading the letter.

I kept scrolling and scrolling. *Okay, where is my name?* I should be down at the bottom here somewhere. I got toward the top of the list and sure enough, I was all the way at number sixteen. I was totally shocked but extremely happy for a minute. But then reality set in. *Okay, there's no way I'll make it through the rest of this. This is just a little teaser.*

I was scheduled for an interview with two detectives from the Waukegan Police Department. It was about as intimidating as anything I had ever done.

I got clean shaven, cut my hair, and had to borrow a suit from my pops. They went at me hard about my family and especially about my gun charge and all the police contact I'd had since childhood. They were reading right off the police report for my gun charge and I told the truth, for the most part…

I remember them asking me if the gun was ever loaded while I concealed it and I was like, "No, Sir."

A lie. I hoped my body language didn't give me away. I felt so cornered and was living in this bubble that there was actually a chance I could get hired and almost double my salary. I felt compelled to twist the truth. All in all, the detectives seemed to genuinely like me and we ended up having a good time in the room together. I walked out of there still holding out hope, although not very much, since I knew a polygraph was potentially coming next.

A couple of weeks later, I heard a knock on my front door and I looked out the window to see that one of the same detectives was at my door.

My heart sank!

One of my family members who Waukegan PD knew very well was temporarily living with me. My beloved brother-in-law, Frank, was my partner and roommate for a while and lived in the basement. I loved him living there and this visit was shockingly unexpected. I tiptoed past the front door without letting the detective see me and flagged down Frank in the basement.

"Man, that detective is here! I think he wants to interview me again about the job."

Frank got this big smile on his face. "I'll hide down here. Just keep him upstairs."

One of the hilarious moments of my life, scheming like a couple of naughty kids. Smuggling Frank into the back of the basement was pretty freaking hilarious. I got Monica out of bed and briefed her on the crisis, and she went right along with it.

The detective was more there to interview Monica than to interview me. He sat down with her for quite a while and then left. On his way out, I'll never forget what the detective said.

"If you pass the psych test, we are going to hire you on."

This unlikely scenario almost seemed to be about to come true. But I still wouldn't get too excited. *There's no way a person like me will ever wear a badge.* It just didn't seem likely. But everything seemed good so I waited for the next letter to come in the mail.

A couple weeks later, there it was. The next magic letter that would take me to the next step. I opened it and read.

Thank you for testing with Waukegan Police Department but unfortunately...

Yeah, sure enough, the powers that be decided that they could not hire a dude with a gun charge who associated with the people that I associated with.

Oh, well... I tore up the letter and went back to work. I admit I was a little disappointed because it seemed like a tease and like I had been strung along a little bit.

But, hey, why dwell on it? There was nothing I could do to change it.

Back to the grind.

ZION

POLICE

DEPARTMENT

A ***few weeks later***, I saw another ad, but this time for the Zion Police Department. The city I love.

I did a little research on it and I learned that Zion Police Department got paid a good deal less than other departments but was still potentially a lot more than what I was making. I asked around and I was also told that nobody wanted to work in Zion because of the high crime volume, lack of manpower, and low pay rate.

I recall an officer telling me that I would be crazy to test for Zion. He tried to dissuade me. I told him it's not like they were gonna take me anyways.

Why not test and then call it a day.

This testing process was a little different than Waukegan's process. The written test seemed a lot harder. I remember walking out of it thinking, *No-way I passed.*

The process went basically the same way with the interviews. I got run through the ringer about police contacts and my gun charge. The Zion detectives seemed a lot more laid back than the Waukegan detectives. They were pretty darn cool, as a matter of fact. I don't remember anything specifically horrible about Zion's process other than I didn't feel like they got as personal with me.

I was a pretty good ball player for Zion High School growing up and a lot of people knew me in the city. I would later find out that my dear friends, Rich Oates, Steve Richter, and Jack Neimi, all Zion school teachers, put in a good word for me. They will forever be included in any good work that I do and I will be forever indebted to them, except for helping them root for their disgusting Packers and Cowboys.

After months of waiting, I finally got a letter from Zion that I made their final list. I was actually dead last on that list. I barely passed the scoring, but I was on the hire list. It felt fake. I was waiting for the bottom to fall out. The whole thing seemed too bizarre to be true.

Matt Thornton, local moron, a copper?

I did not believe it until the day Deputy Chief Larry Booth called me into his office to fit uniforms and to be sworn in.

Wow, I did it. This is complete madness.

Little did I know.

GROUND ZERO

Everyone has such visions of grandeur when they are first hired as an officer.

I was no different.

I remember bringing my family to city hall to be sworn in. When I think back on how ignorant I was about this path I was taking, I chuckle to myself.

Smiling with my kids and family and swearing on a Bible to uphold the law. I even brought my grandmother from Mexico to the city hall with me.

Such a naive twenty-nine-year-old.

That swearing in was almost like stepping into a twilight zone that I have yet to return from. If I could divide my life into a before and after split, this would be the exact moment.

They told me that I would be going to the Illinois State Police Academy.

It would be a three-and-a-half-hour drive every Sunday night to the militaristic boot camp-styled facility. I was given plenty of forewarning about the academy by friends of mine, so I kind of knew what was coming, psychologically speaking.

They march you in like first day recruits in the military.

Try to stress you out.

Stay in your face.

Put pressure on you.

Drill.

March.

5:00 am run.

No freedom.

No talking.

Barracks.

None of it surprised me one bit until the second day when I was singled out in front of the class. The class supervisor had some papers in his hands and began to scream at me. I was so confused because I hadn't done anything at all besides stand there and take direction.

He then proceeded to scream out my weapons arrest so that the whole class could hear it. Not that I was embarrassed, which is what he probably was trying to do. He then went on a tirade about how he doesn't know if I should be there and how I can't be trusted while I'm there.

He screamed all kinds of nonsense and loads of crap in my ear like I was completely beneath him. Now mind you, I am older than this dude and I promise you, tougher than him. I honestly wanted to whoop him in front of the class, wearing his ridiculous military hat like we were in Beirut.

How dare he make such a pitiful attempt to humiliate me.

I'm a grown man with a family.

Wasn't it my city's job to conduct background checks.

I passed.

I was there to learn the job, or so I thought. He then proceeded to put me in front of the class for the next two days in attempts to humiliate me and pressure me into quitting.

This was so insulting to me as a man. I've never understood what degrading another person accomplishes. It didn't make me mentally stronger. It didn't teach me anything. It didn't serve any purpose whatsoever other than fueling me to promise myself that my career would bury his. That attempt at humiliation has never left me; it continues to fuel me.

So, welcome to the profession and my first 48 hours with a badge. I'm still a little bitter about that if you can't tell. I ended up passing the academy near the top of my class and I will never go to Springfield again, thank God. I guess I learned what I needed to down there but I honestly have no fond memories.

A very notable thing I remember about the other recruits at the academy is the lack of basic street knowledge. Not that it was their fault or anything, but it just felt from day one that I was in a different sort of world.

Simple conversations with other recruits showed me that there was little in common with the world I came from and their world. And we're talking about urban officers – officers that are about to go into socio-economically and racially diverse White, Black and Brown neighborhoods, many crime-ridden, many violent, many very dangerous.

I got along very well with all of my fellow recruits but to be honest, I was very surprised by seeing nothing that I would perceive as street experience. I remember very basic things they had to be taught about gangs, street slang and minority culture. It was absolutely shocking to me.

They had to be taught in a classroom about these things.

It was so foreign to me. I really figured there would be other people like me there – people who weren't necessarily squeaky clean and had experience being in trouble and being around trouble.

I remember having to explain to many of them what, Five-0, one-time, folks, people, bond court, and other rudimentary things that I figured everyone knew simply because that was the field they were going into.

I totally misjudged that.

I think that is one of the biggest issues nowadays with policing.

Police recruiting tends to look for the lily-white, squeaky clean guys and girls. This MUST change. Too many people are disregarded when applying for policing jobs from a past transgression. I understand certain crimes that you cannot come back from, but some rejections of applicants are simply ridiculous.

You should see how many messages I receive from dejected adults who want to make an impact in the policing world but are turned away because of petty indiscretions they had in their youth. I am convinced that people with some dirt on their record in the past make great cops. It's so much easier to place yourself in a so-called violator's shoes if you've actually walked in them.

I am a big advocate of people from a neighborhood policing that same neighborhood. There needs to be more of this.

I know it's hard to recruit cops in the urban areas because of the stigma placed on the profession. But hey, why rest and not fight to change that?

DEMOGRAPHICS

Let me explain a little bit about Zion, Illinois, located in Lake County, right outside of Chicago. It is a city of just under 25,000 people, most of whom live below the poverty line. Out of all of the citizens in our county, Zion has an estimated 35% of the Section 8 public housing residents.

That means a lot of single-mother homes and a lot of inner-city Chicago transplants.

The demographics when I was growing up were about half White and half Black. It has since moved to about one-third Black, one-third Hispanic, and one-third White.

I love Zion as it has always been a melting pot of diversity. Many kids with nothing rub elbows with kids with a lot and we all seemed to get along for the most part.

Zion does have its share of violence and drugs. Zion is ranked in the 90th percentile per capita in burglaries, shootings, and robberies compared to other cities our size. Being a cop in Zion, you will experience everything there is to see in a very short amount of time on the job.

I have been involved in countless murder, robberies, rapes, and burglary investigations.

I've been shot at.

There have been at least five officer-involved shootings since I have been on the job.

We have been in countless high-speed chases.

I've tased countless people, been in knock-down drag-out fights, and I could go on and on.

I'm trying to paint a picture of what working in our city is like. I recall my very first night working the road. I got a call over the radio of a subject who just rammed some officers in the city next to Zion. We were assigned to look for him on a stretch of road leading to our city. The radio message was as follows:

"Be on the lookout for……. Use extra caution because the subject just said today that the next cop who approaches him will be shot in the face…"

This was my very first night.

I remember puckering up a little bit and thinking of my kids, Monique and Junior, who were six and four at the time.

I can honestly say that I was nervous.

Now looking back at it, this was just a run-of-the-mill call that wouldn't even catch my attention or get my blood flowing at all if it happened today. You just get used to things like that. I have seen more people die in front of me then I'd like to remember. But our brains have this mechanism where if you see something, you cannot un-see it. The picture of the incident will always be there somewhere in your head.

There are a few that haunt me daily. Mostly the dead kids and the few adults who died looking right into my eyes. Those bother me still. I've never been able to shake those memories.

ROOKIES

N*ow any cop's rookie* season will undoubtedly be the most stressful.

It's such an unknown.

You question yourself about your every decision.

Things come at you fast.

You're always in fear of how your field training officer is going to treat you.

Certain officers refuse to talk to you, a totally bully punk move.

This one particular officer got under my skin. Looking back at it as a 18-year veteran, I can't imagine myself being mean to someone just because I can get away with it. I have a term for dudes like that.

They have the "I'm hung like a light switch" syndrome.

The obvious over-compensation of "wanna-be" toughness was always so easy for me to see right through. This is their only way to feel superior.

Yes, I am intentionally trying to offend you in writing with this, you clown bullies. Knock it off! If this applies to you, don't admit it out loud.

My very first night as a rookie included a guy that threatened that he was going to shoot me in the face if I pulled him over. Those types of things just start to eventually blend together. You simply get used to it. After a while, it hardly gets your adrenaline running at all. You get used to living on edge and thinking about death.

The reality is that every call you go to, there is a real possibility that you may be sued, harmed or killed.

The days and nights just blend into one another.

You're given the most difficult and heartbreaking cases by your trainer simply to get experience in handling them. The constant theme that's expected is that you should have no emotions, no reactions, keep a poker face, and nothing should bother you.

You are expected to have tough skin and when you see death and carnage, put it away somewhere in your little three-pound brain and move it along to the next call.

This is a repeated pattern minute by minute, hour by hour, day by day.

It doesn't deviate or loosen up.

It's like being in the boxing ring getting hit with a nonstop combination.

You might be waiting for the opponent's arms to grow weary so you can cover up and hit back, but he never stops punching. The bell rings, the break flies by with no real time to get a breather, then the bell rings again to get back off your stool for more nonstop combos.

There's never any time to actually process what you're going through.

I went through some heartbreaking things my rookie season. From having to arrest people who I grew up with and loved to losing friends who now hated me because I was a cop.

I had my personal vehicle vandalized multiple times. I had a person who I had known for many years tell my daughter he was going to shoot me in the head.

I had family disown me for a time because they thought I was coming after them, which couldn't have been further from the truth.

There are the calls I dealt with. People shot, people stabbed, people maimed, people raped, etc. These calls inevitably blend together, however, some linger with me and stick out that were extra horrendous.

One example is when my partners and I found the murdered bodies of two nine-year-old girls.

Then, the very next day, I saw a lady purposefully run down by a vehicle.

What we are expected to do is process the first one overnight. Then move on to the next incident and focus on that.

Heck, I still to this day haven't processed that first one yet. Our brains simply cannot do this without something short circuiting slowly within them.

Then there is the 'getting used to a new identity' phase. You are now known as a cop no matter what.

You can never escape it.

Every party, family gathering and every trip to the store. I still shop in Zion every day. People will mention or ask you about something police related. It's just the nature of people. We are drawn toward criminal-related things. It's a natural curiosity for most people to want to hear about things that go on in the night. I have had my named dropped more in the city of Zion than Trump's name gets dropped on Fox News.

I have officially gotten friends and family out of 1.3 million dollars in traffic tickets (insert angry face).

First off, you better be reading this because you purchased my awesome book! Second off, you better be nice to me or I will rat you out in my next book!

So yeah, that 'Matt's a cop thing', can never really be turned off. You can never really come down from that adrenaline high and be normal. And you never sleep right. You are always on an off shift and getting called in to fill shifts. Now if you put all these things in one full year of nonstop action, eventually there is a milestone you can reach.

That milestone is what my dear friend and partner, Janet Mason, refers to as 'disillusioned with life'. You lose the actual emotions that an average person would feel.

It's like a callus that slowly takes over your existence.

I knew deep down in my mind that these things should be getting to me, but they simply were not. Maybe I didn't have time to dwell on them. Maybe I felt that I couldn't dwell on them because I would perceive myself as weak. Maybe I was so cynical and secretly mad at the 3% of society that I dealt with that I refused to process it.

There are many different reasons that we compartmentalize the carnage. But it eventually cannot stay in the box of our tiny brains. It will eventually come out somewhere. And that somewhere is not usually healthy.

In my disillusioned state, my processing came out in boozing. I would get myself so intoxicated that I couldn't have a care in the world. I also became very dependent on prescription drugs to be able to sleep.

The thought of talking to someone professionally about all the stuff stuck in my brain never crossed my mind for a millisecond. I just accepted the fact that this was going to be how things were going to be and I would be tough enough to deal with it.

Hey, my co-workers seemed fine and I knew I was tougher than those morons, so on I went.

QUESTION FOR THE LADIES

Why in the world does a certain population of women melt over a dude in uniform?

This is something that I never could quite comprehend.

Of course, I am not a woman, so I don't really wanna comprehend it.

Speaking as a dude, I have never seen the mail lady's uniform or the sailor chick at the mall and said to myself, "Ooooh, that's hot. I gotta have that."

But man, there is this segment of women who ogle and give attention to you for no apparent reason other than the uniform. Maybe it's the power factor. Maybe some cops are quite handsome, me being on top of the list (wink-wink).

I think this adds to the personas and egos of cops that they have to maintain this tough facade and act like carnage doesn't bother them. It obviously adds to the immorality factor and the divorce rate.

All in all, this persona is extremely unhealthy. I've seen it end in disaster. This all plays hand in hand with our stresses. Just another thing to fit inside of our tiny brains. These little temptations lead to a distorted perception in which you are not only invincible, but your ego gets so puffed out that your head can't fit through the door.

Who in their right mind would openly admit to mental weakness in this state. It goes against every essence of being a mini-celebrity macho man police officer.

So, we maintain this little world inside our minds with the carnage still coming nonstop.

After the first year is when you start in on new stresses. Court cases start to turn over from all the productive arrests you've made as a rookie. You feel like you've earned enough respect that you can talk about your sergeant when he leaves the room now.

You can sound off about what is bullsh&t in the department.

You can sound off about who you like and dislike within the walls now because you are off of probation. You're free now! You're officially starting your union-supported 20-year march to the finish line. You are officially a 100% vested blue blood brother. This is your identity and anything that poses even the slightest threat to that identity or the progress of that identity through the rank and file will turn you into a paranoid wreck.

You will inevitably have your first write up or false complaint against you. You will act like this does not bother you but there is nothing further from the truth.

You want me to explain how weird your mentality becomes? Any cop can attest to this.

Let the deputy chief call you to come to his office over the radio without an explanation. You turn into an instant mess.

What did I do?

Who complained against me?

Am I in trouble now?

Do I need a union rep?

You panic with all of these thoughts in those few minutes it takes to get up to his office. It seems so unreasonable, but it is so true. I believe the reason for this is that you see an unknown that you can't immediately control and that sets you off. It's territory that makes you completely uncomfortable. It's something that momentarily threatens your identity and existence.

I recall being suspended my rookie season. A guy was running his mouth at us on a domestic call. We arrested and charged him but at one point in the call, my partner, in a comical ploy to scare the guy, told me to turn off my squad camera. I unfortunately hit the off switch. Now we never laid a finger on the dude and he never even said that we did. It was a silly little game to shut him up that I should have known better than to go along with it. When the bosses saw the video cut off, they were not pleased.

But here's where departments add to the paranoia of their officers. I've seen this play out so many times over my career. My chief told me that they would investigate and let me know what my punishment would be when they got around to it. So here I am, this young officer, being held for weeks in limbo.

Am I getting fired?

Am I getting sued?

Am I going to have to look for new employment?

I was a wreck for a month while I waited. Yet, I was expected to still go call to call, put it in my pocket and falsely pretend like it wasn't there. This is a cruel mind game played way too often by chiefs. There is no reason to do this to the mental health of an officer.

Why not resolve it immediately?

I knew and admitted that I was wrong. It was my first negative incident; give me my punishment and I'll honor it. This was not a presidential impeachment that required a month-long investigation. It was a silly incident that shouldn't hang over my head.

But there it is again…

Show no weakness.

Deal with it.

Do your job and shut up.

Bury the stress as far as you can.

I remember not being able to tell my wife what was wrong with me for that whole month.

I had been trained to not talk about it, to put it away.

This could easily be resolved with a little understanding from the bosses. But asking an old timer to change something is easier said than done.

Another thing that you can never seem to turn off in your brain is keeping your head on a swivel and watching out for things 24 hours a day.

It's a hypersensitive paranoia that does not leave you ever.

I remember in my rookie season, being on a mundane domestic dispute. We were about to make this gentleman leave the home because he was drunk and belligerent toward another family member. He was standing there looking at me, and then all of a sudden, he started to reach toward his cargo pocket. As he was opening the pocket, my partner yelled out, "He's got a gun!"

Turned out, he was reaching for it to pull it out and shoot me. I quickly grabbed his hand, hemmed him up and then put him in handcuffs. I then removed the loaded hand-cannon that was in his pocket. Just a drunk old dude who ended up apologizing to me later. But that just shows you how quickly things can swing, minute to minute.

I refer to this hypervigilance as being 'turned on'. It's like a switch that I can never turn off. I try to, but it's embedded in my muscle memory to check everything around me at all times.

A relaxed state is something that I simply long for but can never achieve. As I'm typing this, my four-year-old is asleep next to me on an airplane heading home from Las Vegas. She's wearing an Elsa princess costume that I bought her. She got so many smiles and compliments from strangers all day in the airport and even as we got onto the plane. In my head, I am polite and thank everyone, but the cop in me thinks:

Okay, is this person a molester?

Are they looking at her in an abnormal way?

Should I post these pics?

Will a pervert see them?

In reality, these are completely nice and kind citizens who are offering a sweet compliment to a beautiful little princess. Even still on this plane, I've watched every person who has gotten out of their seat. The first thing I instinctively do is look for their hands. I unbuckled my seatbelt and lifted my armrest so that I can jump up quicker in case something happens.

Why?

I have no idea why.

But I have to.

My logic says, "Knock it off, you moron, and enjoy your vacation," but my cop side says, "You never know."

It's engrained in me. Ask any cop.

Where do you sit in a restaurant?

Back against the wall so that we can see the door.

What do we do when someone rings our doorbell unexpectedly?

Locate a weapon and then answer.

What do we do when we pull into our garage?

Look in the mirror to see if we've been followed.

These small examples are so typical of the fact that you can never relax. Like I said, you have to stay turned on.

You're a protector.

You must save the world.

You must not show fear.

You must not show weakness.

You can never admit to any pain.

All of this from a family dude who simply answered an ad in the paper.

PONDERING LOVE

There was another huge elephant that was in every room my rookie season. This was the realization that most of my fellow officers did not see the world as I saw it.

In the next block of examples, I will hit on things that are not necessarily a battle for the typical officer. However, I believe there are many specific personal battles that every individual officer faces. Let me ask you a couple of questions to ponder.

Have you ever been shown true love by a murderer?

Have you ever been embraced by a gangster?

Have you ever had a dope dealer look you in the eyes and tell you that they would protect you with their life?

Have you ever been lovingly helped by a gang member?

Before I received any badge or authority, I had all of these things happen many times over. So how can I be some hypocrite, holier-than-thou, self-righteous dude and just place my hand on the Bible, be sworn in, and now forget all of that happened?

Those murderers, shooters, gang bangers, dope dealers – they are not my enemy! Now don't get me wrong, I ain't crooked and I've never done anything unethical on the job. I've painfully locked up people I've known and loved since childhood, then went home and sobbed.

One thing that I could never accept when I first got hired was the fact that officer referred to many that I grew up with and loved as vermin. I remember my first week on the job an officer coming up to me and saying, "You grew up with so-and-so?"

I answered affirmatively.

"Well, he's a piece of shit."

I did not know this officer and this was basically my first encounter with him. It seemed that he was likely put up to it by other officers. It shocked me. I have never thought of any human being as a piece of shit.

I'm thinking to myself that I knew my friend was no angel, but I had and still have so much love for him. How do you just urinate on someone's existence like that? Write him off as the enemy who is to be wiped out.

This was a pattern that I saw over and over again., and by people who were not even from the city of Zion that I love. They seemed almost like foreign invaders at one point to me.

Why so much anger?

Why so much aggression?

Why so personal?

Aren't we supposed to be professional peace makers?

If my friend breaks the law, do your job. And believe me, I've locked up many friends over the years. But why so hateful?

He singled me out to snipe vitriol knowing that I was just a rookie who wouldn't say anything back. Let's say that it was a train that I never chose to ride on or even get near. Nobody on earth can influence me to hate another man. I've broken bread with some of these alleged "pieces of shit."

Some of them are so proud of me. Some of them have said, "If any officer is gonna arrest me, I hoped it would be you."

I take these things very personally. It has put me in a horribly strange existence. I don't want any enemies and never intended to have any.

I thought this job was honorable.

THE REAL 45

Every officer is given a body number when they are hired in Zion. Mine was 45. Trump, I'm the REAL 45!

Your body number is the number you listen for so you know you are being summoned to a call. It's the number that makes your ears perk up and there is a small drum roll that goes off in your head.

Is this one going to be a simple telephone harassment, report only?

Is it going to be a violent domestic battery?

Is it going to be a shooting?

We have all of these in Zion.

Click

"45"

Click

"45- go ahead..."

Click

"Start for..."

They give out the address and nature of the call.

We receive dozens of calls per shift and we are extremely busy in Zion. So the up-and-down adrenaline is a constant that you learn to live with.

There is really just a small team patrolling our city at one given time. And when your partner has to take a call that needs a cover officer, it means you are literally alone in the city, unless you wanna count the supervisor. But you'd have to wake him up first, LOL. Okay, I might get killed for that last line. No, but for real, your supervisor will help out too.

There is also proactivity, which means that we make our own calls. I used to be the heavyweight champ of proactivity. My favorite thing was to attack the blocks with the highest drug traffic.

Zion has some of the most brazen, open air drug dealing in the state so this was relatively easy for me. When heroin blew up, I would make multiple drug stops every shift. It was, and still is, our biggest problem so it made the most sense to me to attack it.

One night on the midnight shift I was watching one of our heavy drug traffic blocks. I saw a female in a van pick up a dude at the corner. This was the M.O. for our drug transactions.

Pick up the dealer, drive around the corner while making the hand-to-hand, drop him back off, go shoot up.

So I got in behind the van and saw that it did not signal at an intersection. I put my lights on and the van pulled over to the right. Now on stops like this, I totally anticipate that someone might run from the vehicle. I have been in countless foot chases and many of them were on traffic stops similar to this. Sure enough, right as the van stopped…

Whoosh!

The passenger door flew open and there he went. This is where split second decisions come into play. You can either stay with the vehicle and call out the description of the person running or give chase and let your partners know to hurry and get to the vehicle.

I have always been one of the most explosive athletes on the department. I'm not one of the donut eaters who needs CPR after walking up some porch stairs.

I am actually proud to say that Sergeant Dave Grinhaug is the only person on the police department who is faster than me. We took first and second place collectively at SWAT school during the sprint competition. So of course, I'm giving chase and hawking this dude down. Now he had about a 20-yard head start on me since I had to unbuckle my seat belt and secure my squad door. But I closed the distance within seconds.

I was instantly congratulating myself. In my head, I was picturing myself standing on the podium, about to have my Olympic gold medal placed around my neck.

I was so cool for that twelve seconds of my life.

I was a hero.

I was Superman.

I was Matt the Mighty Street Cop!

Then all at once, I saw the dude do a header over a steel fence. Taser time! Tasers are very effective for stopping people. A little five-second burst, then handcuff, then brag to everyone how you hawked and secured this dude all by yourself. And probably get a felony amount of drugs off of him as well and a nice pat on the back from the supervisor.

I pull out my taser and point it straight at his back and pull the trigger right as he flipped himself on the other side of the fence.

Boom!

I gotcha...... Ummmm... Wait... What... the...

*S&*T! F*&K! F*&*&*&*&&&*&*&***K!*

The worst and longest five seconds of my life. I was stuck and fell forward against the fence. My flashlight fell on the other side of the fence and onto the ground. I was squealing like a stuck pig. My muscles couldn't move. My testicles felt like they were about to explode like a grenade. I was about to poop myself. I couldn't hold it in. Only my eyes could move and I see that this dude flipped another fence and then cut north bound and is now out of sight.

He's gone, scot-free, never to be seen again.

So after the five seconds from hell expired, I look to see that somehow the taser prongs had bounced off of the fencing area and thrust themselves right into my right arm and left hand. The perfect connection for a beautiful electric charge.

In my humiliation and prideless man tears, I wanted a pacifier and my mommy at this point. I picked up my flashlight and let off a series of cuss words that I cannot repeat because my pastor might be reading this.

And if this wasn't disgraceful enough for my manhood, I turn to see the van squeal away. So with tears in my eyes and while sucking my thumb, I hobbled back to my squad. I then saw that my squad camera was on. I watched the tape only one time with full deniability since I did not tell anyone about the folly that I just created.

I reported to my shift commander that the taser had malfunctioned but left out the part where I was screeching like an off-key opera singer with tears and snot running down my face. The simple thought of the years of torment I would have endured if anyone ever caught sight of that squad video was too much to bear. It was the best kept secret of my entire life.

So, boys and girls, what is the lesson from all of this? I think it's twofold.

One, let's outlaw tasers. I never knew a little piece of plastic had the potential to suddenly turn a tough, solid, muscle-bound speed demon into a two-year-old toddler crying for his mommy complete with pablum smeared on his face, a full diaper, and hiccup tears.

Two, when you are the star of a potentially viral video, do not let any cops know! It was the smartest move of my entire career.

PTSD

N***ow I'm no scientist*** or psychologist, but I can tell you what I've lived through and seen others live and die through.

I have done some research and found that there are different types of PTSD. Many books have been written about this topic by people much smarter than me. Everyone seems to make comparisons between military PTSD and police officer PTSD. I used to make this mistake myself.

A soldier at war sees things that are unfathomable and often times, dwarf the amount of carnage that your average urban police officer sees.

The problem is we are comparing apples to oranges.

Hats off to any servicemen, especially the ones who survived war. I really don't know if I could do what you guys did.

You are all my heroes.

Many will even go into law enforcement after their service and I give you a double hats off. There is a very real difference between war time experience and the 20-year experience of a police officer.

I believe that with all due respect to both sides we need to stop comparing the two.

A police officer's PTSD is what I would describe as probably a prolonged, less-intense pain. But the pain can be just as fatal, nonetheless. Walking through life always turned on is something that our brains were not designed to do. There is always going to be a breaking point if the pain is not dealt with in a healthy way.

We officers often have this mentality and way of thinking that we are the ones whose eyes are open, that we know the real world and it's out to kill us. All of the citizens are the naive ones who live in harm's way. We are the one percent who understand.

We need to strike that thinking from the record and admit that we cops are the ones thinking outside of what we should. Being turned on means I really shouldn't stop at this gas station for fuel on the way home.

What if a perp sees me?
What if they see what kind of car I drive?
What if they follow me home?
Really?
Have I become that afraid of the boogeyman?

I recall back in the day at the drive-in liquor store when these Latin Kings were about to light up my car with bullet holes because of who I had in the car with me.

I think of that dude back in the day who had his pistol waiting for me in this chick's front yard because I was messing with his baby mama. Now that was some real danger. I had no training. I had no tactics. I had no gun, that I will admit to. I had no survival experience.

Now that I am trained and experienced, why does the thought of a simple stop at the gas station cause stress?

This is the effect of that slow pain I am referring to. It's a constant little stressor that lingers 24/7.

It wears on you.

It changes your rational thinking of what real danger is. It's that boxing combo that won't stop. Even though it is irrational, it is so hard to rid yourself of.

LITTLE GIRL

One of my least favorite things to investigate are car crashes. I have this large tattoo across my throat that reads *Melanie.*

Everyone asks about it because it's the first thing you notice when you see me. It's probably my most obvious tattoo. People think it's my wife or girlfriend.

Melanie is actually my cousin who was more like a big sister to me. She was the best and most lovable woman who I will ever meet in this lifetime. She planned to be a missionary in Africa. Melanie was two years older than me. She was married with a two-year-old son and was six months pregnant. She was super talented and played the violin professionally in an orchestra.

In 1997, when I was twenty-one and Melanie was twenty-three, she was on her way to play the violin at her friend's wedding when she accidentally pulled out in front of a van after not seeing a stop sign on an unfamiliar road.

She died pretty much instantly, and my life was altered forever. You don't get over something like that. It's twenty-five years later and tears still come on random days when something triggers a memory.

Needless to say, professionally handling accidents is extra tough. Every seasoned cop has story after story of the carnage vehicles cause. But some just stick out and stay with you.

One morning after working the midnight shift, we were just finishing up breakfast as the sun was coming up. We got a call of an accident on one of our side streets. These are slow streets and usually have 'simple fender bender' written all over them. So when I pulled up to the scene to see a van on its side and people screaming frantically, I was taken aback for a second. I rushed to the underside of the van and learned that a toddler was trapped under the van. Some good Samaritans had quickly gathered together to lift the van, just enough for the little girl to be pulled out. She couldn't have been older than two years old.

Apparently, she had fallen out of the window after a small bump from the side. The van had been hit just hard enough for it to tip over. Nobody else was injured but the fall of the van had landed on the girl's upper body. I could see that her mother was holding her limp body. It looked like the mother had been dipped in blood from her waist up. She was screaming this blood-curdling scream over and over again, "My baby, my baby, my baby!"

I can hear it today like I'm still standing there now. Immediate medical care was attempted by my boss, but the little girl kept spewing blood from her mouth. Rescue got to the scene and rushed her into the ambulance and sped away. I've never felt so helpless in my life.

What do you say to mom?

Everything is going to be okay?

Calm down?

There is no amount of training that you can go through that prepares you for this. This is not supposed to happen when a mother is simply making a trip down a side street to drop her baby off at the babysitter's house. It was obvious that the little girl was not going to live. If there is a worse nightmare for a mother than losing her baby in her own arms, I don't want to know what it could be.

I probably picture that lady's face once a day in my own head. If there was a solution or a secret formula so that I could un-see and un-hear that incident, I would pay a fortune to have it.

DISILLUSIONED WITH LIFE

N***ow I am not*** saying the experiences along my path are the standard for every cop's career. But I know for a fact that my path is a common one. When you walk this road for a few years, you reach the point of this chapter's name, *Disillusioned With Life*.

Wow, I have at least twenty more years of this?

There are a lot of random thoughts. The unknown of what will happen. The thoughts that this cop world is partially valiant and partially evil. It was such a confusing time for me. But hey, they pay me a lot of money and I appear to have it all together, so I just rolled with it.

After about four years on the job, I began to really question my purpose in life. By this time, the two worlds that I lived in had collided so much and my life seemed pretty much a blur.

I lost contact with some of my favorite people on earth.

A perfect example is my brother-in-law, Frank. We are the exact same age and we had so much in common. Frank, if you remember was smuggled into the basement when the Waukegan detective popped up at my house. Frank and his family always protected me. I felt safe because of them and we had been family forever.

Monica, Frank and family, I love you all so much and that has never changed. As a matter of fact, the love has only grown over the years. I know that we have been through so much and it molded who I am as a man. I hope the feeling is mutual.

I won't go into many details, but the fam has been through a lot over the years. One day I got a phone call from Frank. He had heard some street rumor that was entirely untrue. He thought that I was somehow going to go after some of the family in a law enforcement capacity, like proactively following them to disrupt their lives.

I told him that this was absolutely untrue, but he wasn't believing me. He gave me a warning and then hung up the phone on me as I tried to explain the falseness of the rumor.

This broke me.

I was so hurt by it.

It was like someone died.

I considered Frank one of my best friends on earth. I had never heard him talk to me like that.

I wasn't angry whatsoever. I was distraught. I was sad. I wanted to cry. I never thought I'd get this job and then lose those closest to me.

I didn't blame Frank at all. I mean, I also didn't trust police entirely when I was a citizen. I saw his point of view but I wasn't some close-minded cop who thought that I'm good - and he's bad for being wrong and misinformed."

I almost hated life at this point. There was a heaviness that followed me after this. I eventually broke ties with the entire family unexpectedly. I believe they all thought this was true. I started thinking hard about the decision to become a cop. My life was getting way too complicated.

It seemed the more I was out in the street, the more I developed this 'I don't give a f&*k' attitude.

Excuse my language. I do not talk like that anymore, but I'm painting a picture of the direction that my mind was going in at that time. I still had all of the same stresses that I listed earlier: death, court, bosses, etc., but there were more additions for me. This darkness that come upon me, I never acknowledged. I toughed it out.

I'm Matt, the goofball cop.

I can bench press 400 pounds.

I'm a macho man.

I get free drinks wherever I went.

I can handle it.

I remember over and over, running into people I grew up with on midnight shift. And it was always in a negative capacity. Arresting former close friends, getting cussed at by them, called a sellout, being ignored when I would show them love.

I would often tell them, "I'm the exact same Matt; it's me."

Rarely would they understand or give me the time of day. I'm not feeling sorry for myself or downing them at all. I just never anticipated it being this painful.

I've always been the type of guy that loved to be loved. I tried to swallow it and brush it off. But deep inside, I just really couldn't. I feel that I am normal for that. Many cops would say, "Well, forget them. They're not your real friends anyway."

But wait a minute…

Yes, they are my real friends.

These are people who protected me.

Friends who took care of me.

Friends who loved me.

I can't brush it off. It means I have no real friends. I have nobody. No family either. Even Frank and them don't like me anymore. So what now? Drop everything and be some blue family? They're the enemy and we're the good guys?

This unaddressed pain just got multiplied by these additional things. I literally felt that I had nobody that would possibly understand. One thing about the rush of being a cop, especially a nighttime cop, is that you cannot simply get off and turn into a normal person. There is no switch that can be flipped when you walk in the doors of your home and greet your family. If left unaddressed, this can quickly destroy your family.

There is a chemical in your brain called cortisol. It is released whenever there is an adrenaline dump, which in Zion, is a nightly occurrence.

This chemical is very interesting in that it is a normal mechanism in your brain to help you survive. But studies have shown that a daily overload of cortisol can lead to insomnia, heart disease, mental health issues, and overall terrible health.

This might not seem like much to the normal person who gets a rush here and there. Try year after year of it with no end in sight.

Also, there's the fact that you don't even know it's happening to you so how in the world can you address it? Nobody really trains you on this. I never heard of it until I was put onto it by a retired officer who had been through many cop suicides. It was fascinating to me but learning about it well after the fact does me no good.

At some point, I began to lose interest in life. In my own safety. In my own well-being. I dove deeper into the bottle, into making the pain go away for the weekend. I began to ignore my wife at home. The arguments and minor headaches seemed so magnified. I became disillusioned with marriage.

I became obsessed for some reason with this darkness that consumed me.

I recall beginning to sink into this abyss of demonic activity.

The music I listened to got fouler.

The drunken antics got more and more brazen.

There was a numbness to and of my existence.

It was like a darkness created this love for sin and foolery. It literally felt like demons flocked to me like flies flock to a piece of rotting meat. There is scripture depicting this actual feeling.

Demons pounced on darkness and sin. For some reason I welcomed it. My marriage became obliterated, and I ended up splitting from Monica. It's still hard to bring up and I will not write too much about it. I think leaving my children and that house was a pain that I still haven't totally gotten over.

The words that my babies spoke to me when I left are for me and me alone. I will just say it felt like a thousand deaths.

With all of the horrors I've experienced policing, I think my divorce hit me the hardest of anything.

There is a reason that God said He hates divorce. The destruction is so powerful; it can tear lives apart in scores of different ways.

My first marriage lasted from 1998-2007. The divorce was during my third year with the police department, in 2007.

To my kids, Monique and Junior, I would like to personally apologize for the sins that I have committed against and in front of you. If I could take it all back, I would. I often cry to myself when I think of Junior who was six at the time saying, "Papi, come back."

It kills me to think about it.

And when my Monique asked for her Christmas present to be me coming back home, it tore a hole in my heart. I hated every second of my divorce. I have never felt like the same man. I love my kids more that I can possibly write here and I felt like I hurt them so badly. Something in me definitely died in 2007.

After the divorce was final, I turned to more drinking and womanizing, chasing things that could fulfill temporarily, but never fulfill anything permanent. That's why Jesus said to the woman at the well, to drink the living water and never thirst again.

Only His water can satisfy our thirst.

I was chasing all of my carnal desires and catching most of them, but it always left me empty and dead inside. There was a period of time in which I did not go more than three days without sleeping with a different woman. This period lasted a couple years.

It was sad. All the sex and women I'd ever wanted, and it left me with absolute emptiness. I felt nothing. Just like Solomon said in Ecclesiastes, "It's all vanity."

My years of complete debauchery spanned from 2007-2013. Nothing and no one could tell me what to do. I worked for a paycheck to go out and spend. I was extremely wasteful with my money. I never invested a dime because I had started to come up with this master plan in which I would not be around to see the age of 40. I knew that I would end up just offing myself.

I began to take more chances in the street. In a lot of weird ways, this made me an effective officer. I would go into the most dangerous alleys and didn't care about confronting, chasing, and arresting dangerous people. I always led my shift in productivity. In the eyes of my bosses, I was a solid, extremely proactive officer. In my own eyes, I quietly wanted out of the pain I was in.

My officer safety was nonexistent most of the time. I would always watch my partners' backs, but not when it came to my own. I wasn't being lazy or aloof. I simply stopped caring what would happen to me. I could not look myself in the mirror anymore.

I'm a loser.

A wretch.

I am broken.

I hurt my babies and for some reason, I am numb.

There were a few examples of when I would stand in front of a door and hope somebody would shoot me from the other side. There were times when I would be off duty in the middle of the night and going into our most dangerous areas, just daring someone who hated police to recognize me and take me out.

I have seen so many gunshot wounds in my career that I lost count. It didn't look that painful to me. A clean hole and my body would go into shock anyway. It didn't scare me whatsoever.

I would think back to my first night and myself, *Man, where is that guy who wanted to shoot me in the face?*

A simple good night of sleep was something that was a distant memory.

THE HUMAN BRAIN

The average human brain weighs about three pounds.

Only a small portion of this organ actually retains things.

For dummies like me who gave 90% of their brain capacity to the football field and boxing ring, the retention category is even less than the norm.

But there are traumatic things that are embedded in my beat-up brain forever.

I remember so vividly those things that most people don't ever see once in their lives.

I'm not talking about the things on TV or the internet. I'm talking about the things you can touch, smell, hear, see up close and personal.

I wouldn't say that I dwell on a particular one or even a handful of particular ones.

I would describe it more so that my traumatic memory is like a big Wheel of Fortune. At any given time of day, the wheel will land on a particular memory, and I will relive it in my head.

The scary part is that there are so many.

One night very early in my career we got a call of two missing girls. Young girls, nine or ten years old.

We take so many calls of kids who runaway or stay out too late, being naughty. But this one seemed odd from the second it came out. We got pictures of these babies and searched for them on foot, with a dog, and in vehicles everywhere. We scoured every wooded area, shed, hiding place that you could possibly imagine in the city. It just didn't feel right. And then boom, it comes across the radio…

"45 – call the desk immediately"

The tone in the dispatcher's voice made it super obvious to me that there was something horribly wrong. Me and my partners were out of the vehicles on foot and my partner had quicker access to his cell phone than I did so he made the call in.

There was only a sentence or two exchanged between them and my partner hung up his old-fashioned flip phone. I'll never forget his words.

"They found them. They're dead."

We had been in a wooded area not far from where we were told they were found. We instantly began to run on the small cement path that winded deeper into the woods.

After a couple of minutes, we could hear the screams from people who had found the girls. I looked in the tall grass where people were concentrating on and saw the two babies lying there.

My brain took a minute to process it and it did not look real at first. They looked like little dolls to me for a few seconds. Then I could see that their tiny little bodies were ashen white and lifeless. I could see that they had been slaughtered in a savage and brutal attack. My Momo was the exact same age as the girls when this happened. As much as I fought it, I was almost forced by some spiritual force to picture Momo in the place of those babies.

I don't know why, but for horrible scenes like this, I always wonder how I would survive if this was one of my own.

It's a horrible, indescribable feeling to see these things.

But we just don't see them and leave.

When you are the first to a scene, you are now married to that scene. You watch over it and document everything and everyone who goes near it. I was there for hours with the bodies.

I saw news choppers start to gather overhead.

I saw more and more investigators coming to the scene.

It seemed like an eternity was spent in those woods.

Then you get debriefed about what you saw.

Then you report to the task force every detail of what you saw.

And not just one task force member.

It seemed like I had to give the rundown to a dozen investigators, understandably so since the scene was so chaotic.

Every one of my own team members wanted to know what we saw. Imagine doing all of this explaining to a hundred different people.

You know how much emotion you can show?

Zero.

None.

Nada.

All I wanted to do was cry but you gotta hold it in. And not just for the time being. No, you gotta hold it in, period. You cannot be the guy who breaks down crying when talking about this stuff.

It's like a phony toughness that you have to display. This is never said out loud, but it is kind of what is expected of you as an officer, especially a rookie officer. I mean, if you can't handle this stuff with a puffed out chest and a straight face, then I guess we hired a weakling.

I distinctly remember trying to go home to sleep after that, unsuccessfully, and then getting up to work another shift full of domestics and drunk calls.

That very next shift I saw a woman get run down purposefully by her boyfriend in a van. I believe she survived but her arm was ripped off. We had to call in a flight for life chopper to get her out of there.

I didn't have a second to process the night before and then boom, right to the next call, and the next, and the next; it never stops.

But whatever you do, don't cry.

ACTIVE WISHES AND GESTURES

N***ow like I've stated***, every cop's walk is not the same as mine. There are many varieties of walks. But they encompass the exact same thing: the stresses that you cannot talk about out of fear of being seen as weak.

The everyday nonstop adrenaline rush.

The spiritual activity that I know for a fact is real.

The total lack of sleep.

I have never met a cop that sleeps like a normal human being. The inability to turn off being a cop when you get home. The broken families and sky-high divorce rate.

How did it come to this?

What in the world happened?

How did I go from a family man, happy to get this different job, to a single, egomaniac, idiot who would indirectly hurt his own kids?

I always own the blame because they were my actions. However, there is so much more that goes into this. There were so many avenues that I could have taken to seek help if I was educated about this stuff.

I will address all of this at the end. I am not on here just complaining. I want solutions and I believe I have them, so keep reading if you've come this far.

****

So where in the world is a night of sleep?

"Sleep sleep, come out, come out wherever you are," in my best Jack Nicholson Shining voice.

I was around six years into the mess when I realized I hadn't slept right since the academy. My going-to-sleep routine had become a ridiculous repeat of insanity.

By the time I was divorced for a while, I lived with my legendary brother, Micah, aka Icemic the Great. Man, I love my brother. My little twin.

I remember when they brought him home from the hospital. Back in those days, 1979, there were no seatbelt laws. No cheesy tickets to write to soccer moms. No offense to the traffic dudes out there.

I stood right up in the backseat and looked down at my mom as she held little Icemic on her lap. He was so tiny. I remember asking my mom why he kept opening his mouth. He must have been yawning but I remember that distinctly. I remember wanting to kiss him constantly because he was my cute little baby brother. No fruity goofy stuff, I just had so much love for my baby brother. He will kill me for writing this but, hey, I'm an honest dude.

I lived in the downstairs bedroom at Micah's house. The infamous 735. My nightly routine had been nicknamed *The Heath Ledger*.

THE HEATH LEDGER

I jokingly called my nightly routine, The Heath Ledger.

Yes, I was the only one who thought it was a joke.

I guess I used twisted humor to cover my pain.

Rest in peace to Mr. Ledger, who died of an overdose. This is in no way meant to mock or belittle him.

I just remember reading some of the meds he was on at the time of his death and my cocktail seemed similar. There was always a mixture of Ambien, antidepressants, pain meds, prescription and or over the counter, and allergy pills. All washed down with NyQuil. No water needed. It was all I could do to get a few hours.

My mind constantly raced and never relaxed.

Those times trying to fall asleep are still vivid.

There was no phoniness or people to entertain. Just me and my ceiling.

I would consistently think about the train wreck that I turned my life into.

I remember telling myself over and over that I was in big trouble with God if I didn't make it past tomorrow. I had somehow had it in my mind that I would bargain with God since it wasn't an all-out, purposeful overdose, so if I died from it, maybe he'd let me slide.

I was somehow able to block out all of the consequences, both earthly and eternal. It was exactly how the Bible described Pharaoh when Moses was warning him.

His heart was hard.

He probably knew what the right thing to do was, but his heart refused to do the logical thing. In my case, the logical thing would have been to seek psychiatric help.

It is at this point where I simply existed.

There was no ambition.

I even used to tell people, "I will never see forty years old…"

They just took my words in stride because I was constantly joking around. They had no clue that I was being prophetic in my own mind. I knew it to be true.

I stopped paying bills or thinking about anything financial for the future. My ex-wife had put an order in to get more of my money. I got the order in the mail and just blew off court. She was automatically granted the extra money and I didn't care. I wasn't going to be around anyways. I calculated that after my divorce that I was handing over about two thirds of my paycheck. It didn't bother me in the least.

Sitting here today, fourteen years later, I am just now seeing my credit recover from those days.

Back in those days, I would stay back and forth with Icemic and with a girlfriend. The girlfriend put up with me here and there in between the times that she would kick me out. She went through hell with me and it's a miracle that she never murdered me, justifiably. There are so many stories that I could share about our tumultuous relationship. However, I have skirted death enough for one lifetime. Those stories are not for publication!

Icemic used to call me Jack Tripper from the old TV show, Three's Company. Every single week Jack would be hip deep in trouble from his own stupidity. That was me all day long.

One of those days after the midnight shift, I went to my girlfriend's house to sleep. I took my Heath Ledger and lay down. As I had done numerous times before, I practiced where I would shoot myself when the inevitable day came. I used to practice with my little Kel-Tec .380 in my mouth.

The feeling of steel touching the underside of my teeth was always very strange. I also used to practice with my .40 caliber Glock. I would put it to the front and back of my head. Sometimes to my ear. I would always be mindful of the fact that the shot could not miss and maim myself. I wanted to be instantly gone and out of this world.

On this particular morning, the Heath Ledger kicked in a little faster than I had expected and I fell asleep with the Glock on my upper chest and pointed right under my chin.

My girlfriend happened to come home on a break and walked into the bedroom to find me. The next thing I remember were the blankets getting yanked off of me like a magician yanks a tablecloth, leaving the dishes in place. She went ballistic. She started screaming at the top of her lungs that she wasn't going to be the one to find me. She was crying, yelling, bowing up to me, and cursing as bad as I had ever heard her. She tried to make me leave but there was no way I could drive that drugged up. She confiscated my guns and left, still screaming.

She was done.

She went right to the Chief and reported, ratted me out.

I couldn't possibly be upset with her for it. I got immediately called to the Chief's office for a meeting. Chief's attitude was a lot different than I expected. He was calm and cool about it, as if he had seen this many times before.

He ordered me to turn my guns in and sent me off to see a series of shrinks. I was to get reevaluated after an extended period of time for counseling. Chief put on the schedule that I had suffered a back injury so as to not cause me the embarrassment.

There was no way possible I could admit out loud that I was weak, right?

****

I wake up in the morning and I ask myself. Is life worth living, should I blast myself? Before I go to sleep at night I ask myself, is life worth living should I blast myself? Look at myself in the mirror and I ask myself, is life worth living should I blast myself. I got problems but too much pride for me to ask for help, so is life worth living? Should I blast myself?

This is the chorus to a song.

It was a song that I listened to obsessively.

Not in the way that you are thinking. Like, you have a favorite song that you play in your car when you are on a drive.

This wasn't like that. This song was a complete obsession. I would literally listen to this song every day. Like eight to ten hours, every day. I know every small little drum, snare, keyboard note, lyric, voice fluctuation in the vocals, every millisecond of that song.

I know that I heard demonic voices talking to me during that song. I really heard them. They would say things like, *Just get it over with. It'll be easy. God will understand. It's not your fault...*

They were pushing me toward death. And I was so attracted to them. I literally could not stop listening to this one song. I was drawn to this darkness like a drug addict is drawn to heroin. I could listen to this song while walking around the house, working out, on duty patrolling, and totally put on a happy face while dying inside.

I would hold entire friendly conversations with family or people in public while dwelling in this song and in this dark place. I became an expert on faking it. Nobody who came across me in public would ever guess in a million years that I was anything but a stand-up happy dude.

A girlfriend, my mom, my Chief, my sister, and my counselors were the only ones I believe knew about my real condition.

There was also one of my co-workers Derek Zaloudek, my beloved Zee. Zee worked with me every night and at some point, had caught on to my odd patterns.

I can't tell you exactly what prompted him to pull me to the side. It was a beautiful gesture. He had pegged me correctly and I couldn't deny it to him. I instantly broke down sobbing the second he said, "Hey, Man, are you okay?"

I believe Zee's action was prophetic in this war against mental health problems in police work. Those five words he uttered were so simple. But we never utter them to each other. Those five words are totally taboo in a police station. It would be a totally awkward and an insulting question to pose to somebody.

Yet, those five words can be the key to saving someone's life.

I will forever be indebted to Zee for that night. We talked for a while, and I promised him I would try to keep fighting. And while that night with the lady in the parking lot was the night everything officially changed for me, Zee approaching me helped me hold on just a little bit longer.

I know that without Zee approaching me, the chances are extremely high that I wouldn't have made it to that night in the parking lot.

EMMAUS SHOOTING

One night while out on patrol, we got a call that someone had a gun and was popping off shots. After a short time of this repetitive type of thing happening, you get used to these calls. On the weekends in our city, they come very consistently.

Once the adrenaline rush hits, I always have a habit of adjusting my bullet proof vest. Maybe it's my little unconscious way of double checking that I won't take one to the chest with a handgun. With a rifle or slug, I'm a dead man but, hey, I signed up for this so.

I drove to where the house reported and I could hear that someone was popping off rounds. I pulled into the alley behind the home and sure enough, there was a young man firing off a gun.

We would later learn that the initial shots were meant for me and my partner who were pulling up at the same time. After his last shot, he bolted for the back door of the house.

He ran in and I followed in right behind him only to see that there was a full-fledged, Kid-n-Play house party going on. Wall-to-wall people, music blasting, and people drinking and dancing. There must have been a hundred people in that living room.

Needless to say, I was definitely outnumbered and immediately shocked. I wasn't exactly getting welcomed looks either. The anger on people's faces that I just barged in felt to me that most were about to say, "Yo, let's get him!" and then they would rip me limb from limb and feed me to the dog.

The guy who shot off the round at us had disappeared into the crowd. It was a surreal moment of fear, shock, panic, and odd hilarity like, "Whoa, how did I just get here?"

Part of me wanted to say, "You know what, I give up. Can I please just have a beer…"

It seemed like the crowd was creeping closer and closer without moving their legs like all the zombies did in the Michael Jackson "Thriller" video. And then a moment of clarity for me came like a quick blast of wind.

In the crowd that was about to have me drawn and quartered someone said, "Hey Matt!" in an excited and loving tone.

I peeped around the crowd and saw that it was my brother-in-law, Frank.

"Frank!" I yelled out almost like I was drowning and needed him to swim to my rescue.

He immediately came up and gave me a handshake and a hug. Apparently, the music had been loud enough that people were totally oblivious to this dude who shot at us. I then saw other familiar faces of people who I grew up and hung with for years.

Yes, my crazy life. I get a round popped off at me by partygoers who love me. What can I say? I'm honored, I guess.

I was sarcastically offered a drink that I had to politely turn down. Of course, we never found the guy who popped off the rounds.

My guess is that he ran through the back door and right out the front door of the house to get away. Frank apologized furiously and I had to put in the odd request of, "Can you please tell your friends not to shoot at me?"

I really could not make this stuff up if I tried.

The thing is, I can never get angry at those who love me. The streets are the streets. I can never convince the streets to love the police but by my love and actions, I can convince them to love me and then convince them there are many others, just like me.

FINAL PLANNING

Have you ever seen a suicide scene?

Most people, other than police can't say that they have.

If done with a handgun, it can be very bloody. There is a lot of blood and it's stinky and messy. The smell of that much blood never leaves you and a police officer knows that stench of it the second he steps near a scene.

I had a different plan. I had seen this before and for some reason, it never made sense to me. I wanted to leave a clean scene, so I was going to wrap a towel around my head. The only problem I had was figuring out was where the bullet would go. If I put a towel on, I would have trouble seeing the side head shot.

If I went under the chin, I would have to press hard and the angle would be difficult if I was going to use my usual finger to pull the trigger.

I used to practice often in the mirror and finally decided that under the chin was the way to go. The towel would make it easier for Icemic when he found me. I was definitely gonna have to do it at his home.

My girlfriend had been completely done with me and I hadn't talked to her in months. The plan was to leave my iPad open to the suicide letter I composed, make a couple of calls depending on who answered their phone, then get the towels, lay on the bed and finish it.

The climactic ending felt like it was approaching as fast as Carl Lewis down the home stretch. I've experienced first-hand the steps to the end.

You go through this extended darkness and contemplation of killing yourself and it's like you see no hope. And then your hope becomes death itself. The prospect that you will be out of this pain and have no more stress is welcoming in a demonic way. You somehow convince yourself that everything will be fine. After convincing yourself of this, you somehow find comfort in the darkness.

The closer you get to the end, you almost seem a little happier because you know it's going to end.

It's what I started convincing myself of.

This convincing started sporadically over the course of time. Then it became weekly, then daily, then hourly. I would think about this problem or that stress or this headache and then comfort myself by thinking, "Well it's okay 'cause I won't be here anyway."

This convincing started to eliminate my stresses. It replaced them with a finish line. The one thing that I could not stop though, was thinking about Momo and Junior. This would make me instantly cry. I truly believe that the Lord was putting their little faces in my head at certain times to stall my sociopathic plan. When I thought of them it would be instant tears. The thought of my babies slowed me a tiny bit, but definitely did not stop the plan.

There were a few last straws for me.

There was a financial situation that I unwittingly thought I was in legal trouble for.

In retrospect, I didn't break the law at all. It was my own misunderstanding of financial paperwork that I since corrected. But at the time, it scared the heck out of me thinking I could have done something potentially outside of the law. I was a hundred percent sure that I would never last a second dealing with that. If I was contacted about that paperwork, I would have hung up the phone and walked straight to that bedroom with the towels.

I thank God that it avoided me, especially after learning it was all my own ignorance.

The other thing that was going to spell the end was if work gave up on me.

There were so many people who had been proud of me for becoming an officer. If I lost my job, I would have lost my purpose. I could never go back to being a civilian.

I would have had to disappear from sight, which I could not possibly do, or just be dead.

I was going to choose the latter.

Now let's be perfectly clear. I did not mention these triggers to my suicide as an excuse or to soften the fact that I was out of my mind, totally self-absorbed, and depraved. I am explaining what was in my head back then.

I now own my sin.

These triggers were seemingly happening right in front of my eyes. If the span of my life was a football field and the end zone was the end, then in my estimation I was at the one-yard line. I was done with hope. It did not exist. Nothing any human could tell me would phase me whatsoever.

Those shrinks that the Chief sent me to, God bless them all. I love them dearly and they helped explain to me a lot of why I was losing my mind.

However, I knew the right words to say to get out of their office. I'm a professional and I'd been trained and experienced in what not to say to a shrink. It's simple, honestly, which makes it pretty scary as well. I cried to them all and they did their best. It just wasn't enough for me.

I was thirty-seven years old.

I was tired.

I was a scumbag.

I was broken.

I was hopeless.

I was about to do a quarterback sneak into that end zone.

Who would have known on a cold, miserable night, the Lord would send one of His angels to save me in a parking lot.

Matt and Marina (the woman who saved him from himself)

BUN B
MURDER

Investigating murders is something that happens often in Zion.

Whenever I speak with someone who is unfamiliar with my city, they always ask things like, "Have you ever seen a homicide?"

They are always shocked to learn that I have seen more than I can personally recall. The examples I'm giving are simply what come to mind as I'm writing. There is really no rhyme or reason for why I picked these but I wanted to share them for a look into the mind of an officer.

Years ago, we had a typical Chicagoland snowfall, late in the night. It's really the only time that snow looks beautiful to me. I detest wintertime, but snow late at night seems peaceful and it always seems so quiet as the snow falls. There is nothing disrupting the perfect layers that it leaves on the ground because the only people moving in the fresh snow are us night owls, patrolling.

We were all doing paperwork in the station when we got a frantic call from the dispatcher. They advised that someone was standing over another person shooting him execution style.

We jumped right up from our desks to head in that direction. I recall one of my partners starting to run in the station towards the exit. He slipped and his feet got about five feet in the air while taking an embarrassing fall. This was due to the immediate tension he created within himself.

He had total tunnel vision, forgetting that he had just walked in from the snow. I am always a big advocate of remaining as calm as possible. I never run to my squad. I definitely speed up my walk though every time.

Other officers will say what they want and I've gotten some ribbing for being the last to jump in the car. But I learned in the ring that when you speed things up too much, the tension has many different effects on your system.

The number one effect is on your breathing. Your most important function is getting oxygen to your brain. When you speed things up, this inevitably means that your breathing speeds up. When your breathing speeds up your body fatigues quicker, loses focus, and ten ses up. I've had a lot of ring experience and this is why when you watch professional boxers fight, it appears as if they are loose and calm the entire time. Tension creates mistakes and zaps your energy almost immediately. So you will always see me walking quickly and constantly taking deep breaths.

We begin the wagon train to the scene that was about a mile away from the station. We're told that the incident is actively occurring in an alley. I pull into the alley and see this truck with its door hanging open. The truck is parked in a parking space behind a home. The snow is fresh to the point that there is one set of tire tracks and you can see the path that the truck had taken.

From the truck I can hear the familiar voice of Bun B, one of my all-time favorite rap artists. I grew up listening to his music, and in my opinion, he is one of the most talented and charismatic artists ever.

As I walk to the side of the truck by the driver's door, I can see this large man, down in the snow. The freshness of the snow makes it look like one large mattress. I then instantly see the distinct red of the man's blood absorbing the whiteness.

I walk up to him and see that he is struggling to breathe. I can see that there are a bunch of bullet holes in his chest area. He looks at me with wide eyes.

"Stay down, Brother. We got help coming fast."

He then begins to roll around gasping for air like a fish that was just removed from water.

His large eyes still wide open and looking so desperate.

Those eyes are something that I replay daily in my head.

I felt so helpless.

As I walk back to look at footprints that left the area in the snow, the man utters to my partner a mysterious sentence that I hadn't been able to decipher.

Then he clearly says through his gasping, "Can I die now?"

It almost seemed like he was asking permission to leave this earth. Like he tried his best for us to stay alive, but he just couldn't do it anymore and was now giving up his spirit.

I wanted so bad for him to hold on.

There was no reason that he deserved to have that many shots in him.

He had a mother and father.

He probably had kids who loved him.

He was just like me.

He was in an alley that I was familiar with growing up.

He listened to Bun B.

We probably knew and hung out with a lot of the same people.

It was so heart wrenching to see, smell, hear, touch. A few seconds later, his eyes shut and everything went quiet.

I pray that he made peace with the Lord during those final moments. I often think about his mother receiving the phone call. I often wish I knew the Lord back then because I would have prayed with him right then and there.

It's something I do a lot these days…

After all of the chaos subsided, we ended up catching the culprits the next day. I knew the kids who did it.

I liked the kids who did it.

I take that back…

I love the kids who did it.

I'd just got done having a long conversation with one of them. He hugged me. He told me that he respected and cared about me and appreciated me. I cannot comprehend what possessed him to do something so horrible. I couldn't even be angry at him. I was just heartbroken that this happened. I almost wished that the culprit was some deranged, psychotic, southside-of-Chicago visitor to Zion whom I could demonize.

I hated that I knew and loved the kids who did this.

It made things hurt so much worse.

It made me lose hope in life.

It made me lose hope in what was real.

It made me lose hope for anyone I have a pleasant conversation with thinking that they are on the up and up.

This one got to me.

Sitting on the stand for the trial. Watching the mothers of all involved crying and not being able to stop it or even speak to them. I wanted to hug and cry with everybody.

But you can't do that.

You must remain robotic.

No opinion or feelings.

Just the facts.

It's the same song and dance. Get called a liar by an attorney and walk out to work another shift.

I've never spoken about these things.

I guess this is therapy for me.

SOLUTIONS

Now I never wanted to write as if I only had gripes and nothing else to offer. I have been through and seen enough that I can honestly say I have a decent gauge on what could help officers deal with the stresses of the job.

I do not think the public knows how much training an officer goes through. As I wrote about earlier, we all go to the academy which is basically watered down bootcamp.

We train every day for months on the job. Much of the time is spent on tactics on how to stay alive. Verbal tactics, physical confrontation tactics, driving tactics, shooting tactics, stabbing tactics, talking tactics, you name it we train on it.

And this training doesn't stop with the academy graduation.

Departments do quarterly training, firearm quals, tactical response training, more driving training, hand-to-hand training. This goes on for the entirety of your career and is mandated by the state.

All in the name of staying alive while serving the community.

But when it comes to mental health and personal well-being training, up until recently, it was largely ignored. If there was a mental health training to be had it was a fifteen minute briefing at an academy class or an article the chief made everyone fake like they read.

It was not stressed or even talked about other than to maybe denigrate the 'weak people' who 'can't handle the job' and need to 'go do something else'. I've heard it a million times. I've seen guys get ostracized for caring and for doing the absolute no-no of police work, which is getting emotionally involved with a case.

I've wanted to scream for so many years in the face of this madness.

"Are you f&*king human beings!"

How in the world can you not get some sort of emotional involvement over the death and destruction of fellow human lives?

I'm not saying you befriend and walk life with every person you come across. I'm saying, why don't we just be honest about what is bothering us.

I am human,
Aren't I?
I am not a sociopathic psychotic loon who has no human emotion, am I?

Let us cut through the BS and talk about this stuff.

BIAS

POLICING

I remember being in a training class and we were being instructed on bias policing. They asked us to list out the top five attributes of a good officer. On the top of my list, I put the word compassion.

The instructor of the class read it and openly laughed at it.

He then tried to put me on the spot by calling me Mr. Compassion and insinuated that I was as soft as a pillow in an attempt to embarrass and get me to rethink what I wrote.

I stood my ground and had a long productive dialogue with the instructor. I forgave him and I think I may have even had an impact on how he looked at things.

And by the way, this instructor was a chief from a different department. So when you have a chief balking at compassion, I think it is an example of the issues in our police culture. But this anti-compassion is an accepted attitude of most badge wearers from my experience.

There are exceptions, but one day I hope to call some big-time attention to this 'blue Kool-Aid drinking' problem we have.

This attitude should be eradicated!

Like gone!

Like put to rest forever!

It's sickening.

It's against the oath we swore to.

Why is this lack of compassion a quietly accepted fact in most PDs?

There are also more sides of police work that I could not stand. This was the cultural side.

And when I say culture, I'm talking about the blue culture. It seems when you take on a badge, Blue turns into your new ethnicity. There are certain commandments that are subtly pushed on you when you enter these gates. The blue attitude that it is us, the good guys, against them, the bad guys.

I never bought into that mind set from day one.

I think the biggest problem in our police community is that we are never honest about certain things. So allow me to set the record straight.

Yes, this country's policing was founded largely on principles of racism and oppression.

There, I said it.

It's not too hard to figure that out.

It's a fact.

I don't know why we just can't say it, rebuke it, make sure it stays gone forever, and then move on.

Instead, we have this blue pride in which we have always been these untouchable heroes to ourselves, which is so phony to me.

Black people could not even freely vote across the country until 1965.

Jim Crow was real.

People from past generations who still walk around today have felt it. The way people of color have been mistreated over the years is disgraceful and put a black eye on our profession.

Why can't we just acknowledge this and fix it?

Do you know how we fix the perception of hate?

It's sure not by hiding behind a blue wall or buying into the blue culture. It is simply by loving people. I refuse to let anyone dictate who I can and can't be loving toward.

I was saved by the One who is love. I was a criminal in His eyes, a filthy sinner, undeserving to even utter His name. So who am I to judge any fellow human being.

If you're a criminal, I love you.

If you're an addict, I love you.

If you punched one of my coworkers in the face, I love you.

If you're a sex offender, I love you.

My job is not to judge you in any way shape or form. I work for the citizens. If they see me, they are supposed to feel safe. I will do my job correctly and when I must arrest, I will do so. But I will do it with the utmost respect leaving most of the people I arrest thanking me afterward.

There's a certain way to do the job.

Sadly, showing zero empathy and treating violators as if they are of a lower class than us is par for the course, if not encouraged in most places from my past experience.

From day one of the academy, they teach you that a violator is the enemy and if you can't see his hands, he will kill you. It's quite a lot of sensationalism.

Yes, we should be safe.

Yes, we should use good tactics.

Yes, police get shot sometimes.

But we do not get shot to the point where we need to be yelling at soccer moms and Florence Hendersons to show us their hands. I believe police training has to be restructured asap. Police brutality has been overlooked and tolerated far too long.

When I first started this job, if you got into a foot chase with somebody, it was pretty much accepted that the person running was going to get extra when they were caught. It was not exactly condemned. And if you didn't adhere to this, many would see you as weak.

Again, this is something I never tolerated, bought into, put up with, dished out, and so on.

This was always so disgusting to me.

I mean, what separates you from a criminal if you think you have the right to physically harm another person unjustly?

It's sickening.

You may be lying if you say you've never heard old timers talk about what they used to get away with before all these cameras.

Stuff like that contributed to my depression and made me feel disgusted that I wore the same uniform. After I made it clear early in my career that I would not participate in any of this crap, guys just wouldn't do it in front of me.

I have no problem snitching whatsoever.

Then the rumors got around that I wasn't one of the guys or I was weak, I wasn't a team player, yada, yada, yada.

I don't want any part of that team so I thank you for ostracizing me.

All of these philosophical differences at work made my mental health even worse.

I got kinda tagged as a soft guy because I didn't like hurting people. Kinda ironic since I was an excellent fighter in the ring and pound for pound, probably the strongest and most explosive athlete there.

I had many nights of dream after dream of getting some of these guys into the ring.

Like my boxing coach, Coach Danny Nieves would say in the last thirty seconds of a round, "Take him out, son."

If I sound a tad bitter, then, I guess I'm a tad bitter and still need to pray for divine help in dealing with this. I constantly battle with showing grace to officers who have crossed the line.

But I know that's what Christ didn't mention as a suggestion. He stated it as an order.

I must forgive.

I love them too.

YOU ARE NOT THAT TOUGH

Why do recent studies show that there are nearly twice as many officer suicides as there are line of duty deaths?

Why is it that as of six months before writing this, I was never aware of that?

Why did nobody ever talk about this?

It's almost like finding out someone had a key to releasing all my pain that entire time and they purposefully withheld it from me.

It discourages me when I think about it.

Because of some phony facade of toughness that we try to maintain, many have died. That's kind of the way I see it.

Out of all the solutions I can offer, the number one solution is to realize how tough you AREN'T.

I have always said that we do this job with our humanity and NOT with our manhood.

When I first started my career, the predominant mindset was that the toughest cop meant the best cop. Like he didn't take any BS from anyone and was the one you wanted behind you in a fight.

That is such a false way of thinking. Number one, this is not a job to get into for fighting anyone. Of course, you should always be mentally and physically prepared for a fight, but that is the last thing you should ever want to do.

Fighting and going hands on should and BETTER be your last resort.

We have been equipped with enough tools that we should be able to use words in most cases to bring someone into compliance.

It's no coincidence that these 'tough guys' are always the ones in the middle of lawsuits, firings, and headlines.

I've found that these guys are also the ones who aren't really tough at all. They are tough with those who they can be tough with. And I believe the technical term for that is BULLY. I think a perfect example of a true tough guy is one of my partners.

His name is Bart Palazewski.

I've become very close to him since he was hired. I noticed that Bart had cauliflower ears when we first hired him. I remember thinking that he must have been a fighter, so I inquired.

One of my partners simply said, "Google him," so I obliged.

And, oh my goodness, did his name come right up on Google.

Bart is a retired fighter. And I don't mean a guy who fought in small clubs. He was on Pay-Per-Views, like Knockout of the Night by Dana White, yes, UFC Dana White.

Bart is a legitimate bad ass. Like world-class. He has beaten world champs, held titles, put great fighters to sleep.

I would eventually do some light training with Bart and I can attest that I have never seen a striker hit quite as hard in person, and I've been in lots of fighting gyms.

But here's the thing about Bart – he is the kindest, most soft spoken guy you will ever meet.

He loves people.

There is not a cocky bone in his body when he is on the street.

He is humble on the job.

He is respectful to all.

You would never know in a million years that this guy could literally kill most everyone reading this with his bare hands.

Even on the street he doesn't give in to the typical, 'you're only tough because you have a badge' nonsense we hear all the time.

I've seen him literally just smirk when they give him that line. I have actually tongue-in-cheek shown the neighborhoods his footage.

"Um, yeah, you really shouldn't use that line on Officer Palazewski."

The streets get a kick out of that one and the predominant, wide-eyed response is usually, "Oh wow, Matt, we ain't fu&*n' with him."

My point in explaining this is, let's drop the phony tough guy routine.

It's a false façade.

It's like a paper-thin wall that cannot stand.

The more you put on a tough outer appearance, the more you show that you are hiding the pain.

Me and Bart confide in each other about the stresses and the pain that go into this job. We admit that neither of us are tough enough to handle all of this alone. That's a true start to keeping your mental state in the right frame.

I am weak, you are weak, so let's be weak together and walk through this madness together.

VETERANS, WE GOTTA DO BETTER

It has been the long tradition of police work to put the rookie officers through the ringer. To be honest, it was extremely brutal for me.

It's been eighteen years and I would be lying if I said that I don't still feel some sort of way about it.

There is still residual anger that I need to repent of.

As a man, there were, and still are, some officers that in my eyes, deserved to be whooped for the way they treated me.

It was uncalled for.

It added so much unneeded stress in my life.

Like my kids didn't have a real man as a father because he was a rookie?

Like as the leader of my family I didn't deserve the same respect as them because "I hadn't earned it."?

I was less of a man because they happened to get hired before me?

All of it is trash.

That's why I call it the light switch syndrome.

I'm sure those veterans who bully rookies are hung like a light switch. The irresponsibility behind that behavior is reprehensible to me. As a rookie walking into this job where you see inhumane things almost daily in some cities, you should get nothing but positive support.

Of course, there should be a space for rookies to prove that they belong in this profession. But let that stuff come from experience on the street.

Veterans should be taking these kids aside and making sure their heads are okay, that they are handling things well.

Their lives literally depend on this. Just last week there was a horrific death scene that we were involved with. Literally, brains blown out and splattered. A rookie in training on the scene was there. I intentionally took him to the side and said, "Look, seeing this stuff ain't normal."

I made sure he was okay.

I made sure he knew that he could talk to me about it.

I made sure that he knew that we cannot hold this stuff in and that he needs to find a healthy way to unpack it.

I told him everything that I wished someone would have told me.

It's quite simple and it's not complicated.

The danger comes when you dehumanize the carnage and think that you can just deal with it. It piles up fast and it does not stop. It's like an assembly line of horror that just keeps coming.

You need to slow the line down and know where the emergency stop button is on the conveyer belt. Most veterans are so into getting through their careers or just plain bitter and have no time. This needs to be a team effort. I cannot stress this enough: be intentional. If everyone is mentally healthy from the most junior to the most senior, then the entire team wins.

WE
NEED
TRAINING!

I've already mentioned that I never had any exposure to this stuff until long into my career. The mandated training we have historically had in this profession is redundant and so tiresome.

I mean, we literally have daily training bulletins that we have to sign off on.

For a technological moron like me it is nearly impossible to keep up with all of the e-mails about new training links to click and complete. It's almost laughable how much there is.

Yet, out of all of this training, I rarely see anything related to solutions for mental health issues. You might get statistics or scenarios or case laws but rarely anything helpful in dealing with suicide and depression.

I would think this should be ***Number One*** on the list.

I help in teaching a class once a month that is educating officers on just that. And let me tell you, cops are the toughest audience to teach by far. So much cynicism and eye rolling to deal with. That's that phony tough facade that I always refer to. A perfect example of this came in a recent class I taught.

I was scheduled to handle the second hour of training for the day and I was a little early to arrive. I stopped in the bathroom before the I went into the class. While I was in there, I could hear two officers walk in talking to each other.

They had blatantly walked out of class because of the teacher who went before me. I overheard them saying how much they hated this 'training bullshit' and how cheesy and unnecessary it was. It was your typical tough guy ramble. Like, they would rather be out cracking skulls than being in class. At least that's the impression I got with the typical 'F word' being used four times a sentence.

I walked out without being noticed by them but I caught a glimpse of their faces so I could see who they were. They walked into class right after I began my hour of teaching. They sat in the back of the class. So, I go into my teaching, explaining what I endured as an officer and the self-destruction that I caused in my own life. I went through the story and told them how close I was to taking my own life.

As I was teaching, I took a glance back at one of the cops who was in the restroom earlier. His face was bright red and tears were streaming slowly down his face.

It was so obvious to me that his mentality was a result of his pain. His anger and resentment towards the training was simply a defense mechanism. I was overjoyed to put a small dent in that facade.

He came up and hugged me after the class, thanking me. It was one of the more satisfying events that I have seen in a while. I told him that I loved him and that I was here if he ever needed anything. That's the guard that can come down through training.

I believe that our Crisis Intervention Training should be mandated in some way, shape, or form for all police officers.

It should be done consistently and annually.

It literally saves lives.

I couldn't possibly have enough time to tell you about all the feedback I get. Cops will call or message me saying, "Man, I am going through that same thing…" or "I'm so happy you said all of that out loud!"

This should be the norm. Police chiefs, I'm talking to you!

Do you really love your men and women?

You MUST consider this.

CHANGE THE MILITARY MENTALITY

One thing that has always bugged me about this profession is the military mentality. In one sense, I understand it. You should be prepared for a confrontational situation. You should know how to deal with a threat. You should be trained with non-lethal and lethal weapons and prepared to act when you need to.

I get it.

But I've always wanted to scream loudly that I am not at war! I am not a soldier!

Many like to use that analogy. I've always detested it. To be honest with you, from what I've seen over the years, it's not the ex-military guys who try to be 'military' in the job.

It's the non-military guys who try to act like wannabe soldiers that pour on the GI Joe nonsense. Frankly, it's a bit embarrassing to be around.

This mentality carries the assumption that certain citizens are the enemy. It breeds so much fear mongering that is so ridiculous to me. Coming out of the academy, you would think that I was going to face the Viet Cong when I started on the street. I believe that this mentality creates so much unneeded stress for a young officer.

I grew up in my city, so I already knew the culture there. I am the exception to some rule. But you take a kid from a White neighborhood who may not have ever interacted with a Black person before, and you send him to the academy where he is taught that everyone who isn't showing their hands is going to kill them. Then they come back like little paranoid schitzo-wannabe soldier.

That's not an exaggeration either, folks. I've seen it more times that I can count. It is the recipe for disaster. The mental health effect that has on someone can be lasting.

It can also lead to bad shootings because of the mentally stressed 'little paranoid schizo-wannabe soldiers' panicking unnecessarily.

The mentality that we are in some sort of war is more harmful than one book can explain. I know there are many who will disagree but I just wanna ask them, "Ummm, how's that nonsense working out for ya?"

We are hated more in this country now than any time in history.

The shift back to community policing desperately needs a comeback.

And I mean true community policing. Not simply having an officer in the school or a DARE officer.

I mean officers who have a direct effect on the city they work in, on and off duty.

Officers who truly love the city they work in.

Officers who do their job right and consider nobody to be their enemy.

No more, Us vs. Them.

You will always hear the statistics about 98% of the community being law abiding citizens and only 2% are a danger.

Well, if that's true, then let's act like it.

Training is way too fear based.

We receive almost zero impactful training about unity and being ambassadors for the city we work in.

I love to use the term, Professional Peace Maker.

This mentality should be pushed from the second a recruit is hired. The focus should be about making people feel safe when you're around. That is so far from reality right now and I can personally attest to that.

I still get nervous around police. I know how they've been trained. I know many have so little street experience and have been trained that everyone is going to kill them.

They should not have this horribly stressful mentality. It is so far from reality and so destructive to the everyday mental health of a person. Why do we intentionally create this fear and stress?

The depth and lasting effects this has runs deep and I believe costs lives to suicide and destruction. There has to be some compromise and calming of this fear mongering. I see my little sister and my niece, who are both about 4'11", with zero training, zero guns, zero tasers, zero backup, driving in and out of our toughest blocks constantly taking care of our needy families.

They show zero fear.

And we have sworn officers who are afraid of a take home a squad because some boogeyman might see where they live.

We have sworn officers who refuse to go anywhere near the city they work in because El Cucuy might jump out of a closet and get them.

We seriously need to train ourselves out of this mentality. Chiefs, let's get on this! It will do wonders for the comfort and mental health of the officers.

EVERY SHEEPDOG NEEDS A SHEPHERD

You know what the most misquoted verse I've ever personally seen is?

"Blessed are the peacemakers for
they will be called the child of God."
Matthew 5:9

If you walk into any police station around the country, you will probably see this verse somewhere. Posted on a wall, screensaver, billboard style hangings, buttons, patches, tattoos, etc.

My best guess is this is some sort of uplifting verse that is implying that cops are children of God, because they are cops.

First of all, this is a verse from Jesus' dissertation on the Mount of Olives. The sermon is known as the Beatitudes. During the sermon, Jesus is going through the characteristics of what a follower of the one true God should look like.

Poor in spirit, in other words, remorseful that you are a sinner and need forgiveness.

Mourning with those who mourn.

Meekness or having a gentle spirit.

Merciful, hungering for righteousness, pure in heart.

This is much of the list. In no way, shape, or form was Jesus stating that cops are children of God simply because they are cops.

I can tell you firsthand that during my miserable self-destructive years as a cop I was absolutely not a child of God. The oft quoted, "We are all God's children," is simply biblically inaccurate.

John 1:12 squashes this notion when it reads,

"Yet to all who did receive Him (Jesus), to those who believed in His name, He gave the right to become children of God."
John 1:12

In order to be a true child of God, we must repent and believe in the mediator who is Jesus, and not simply believe in Him like you believe in Abraham Lincoln or some historical figure. True belief is a personal knowledge of Him.

Does He know you?

Do you seek Him?

Do you strive for a relationship with Him?

Is your life's story about chasing after Him and striving to please and obey His commandments?

Those are questions you must wrestle with. And if you are reading this with no desire or belief in anything that has to do with Jesus, no worries. I love you and am simply reasoning with you to seek for yourself.

Cry out and I promise He will answer.

Just like He did for me in that squad on that cold winter night. On judgement day, Jesus will ask everyone a simple question, *Who was I to you?*

I lovingly invite you to the forgiveness and redemption that I found. With all that being said, a knowledge of the true Shepherd is the perfect remedy for any sheepdog who is inevitably struggling dealing with the day-to-day evil that cops see.

It will not guarantee that everything will be good; you will still have many struggles. But it will guarantee that He will show you how to sustain through the turbulent times.

"Come to me all who are weary with heavy burden.
I will give you rest."
Matthew 11:28

This verse literally sums it all up in one simple sentence. And no, I am not turning all religious on you.

I actually am not an organized religious person whatsoever.

I am a personal relationship guy who knows that on Judgment Day, there will be no cover unit.

There will be no sergeant to direct and guide you.

There will be no FTO to help you through.

It will be you alone.

It will be you and the Shepherd, and He will know who you were to Him.

Galatians says, “He is not mocked,” meaning, He knows every thought and desire you have ever had during your time on earth.

I love you!

Consider this, you valiant, beautiful, brave, sheepdog!

The two biggest gifts to my new life -

NOT THE END JUST THE BEGINNING

A***s I mentioned way*** at the beginning of this book, I ended up becoming the adoptive father to hundreds of kids. Well, since I wrote that passage, it's actually become more like thousands. Well in my best goofy voice all I have to say is "well... what had happened wasssssssss......".

You see I kind of started an amazing organization that has become pretty famous. I mean like pretty pretty famous. Like been featured on ABC, NBC, CBS, PBS, and multiple other independent networks.

When the Lord blesses you, my best advice is to just roll with it, shoulder shrug, smile and give Him the glory. I could tell you more about the happenings of my beloved "My Father's Business" organization in this book but I've decided that MFB needs its own book. Stay tuned!!

I have found a new high, habit, vice... whatever you wanna call it. And that is helping at-risk youth. MFB gives Agape love to any youth to try and plant eternal seeds.

There are simply too many stories to list.

Some heartbreaking and some so joyful that I smile ear to ear. The next time you see a book cover from me you will be blessed with some of those stories.

I LOVE YOU ALL!!!!
GOD BLESS YOU!!!!
MT#45

My typical Friday night at MFB…

If you are suffering from depression or having suicidal thoughts, please reach out to a trusted friend or family member and seek professional help.

YOU ARE NOT ALONE!

HELP IS AVAILABLE

National Suicide Prevention Lifeline –

1-800-273-8255

Emergency Number - 911

https://suicidepreventionlifeline.org/

https://www.survivorsofbluesuicide.org/

INSTAGRAM: @InkHeadStudios

Made in the USA
Monee, IL
12 May 2022